GOVERNMENTS, FARMERS AND SEEDS
IN A CHANGING AFRICA

Governments, Farmers and Seeds in a Changing Africa

Elizabeth Cromwell

Overseas Development Institute
London

CAB INTERNATIONAL
in association with the
Overseas Development Institute

CAB INTERNATIONAL
Wallingford
Oxon OX10 8DE
UK

Tel: +44 (0)1491 832111
Fax: +44 (0)1491 833508
E-mail: cabi@cabi.org
Telex: 847964 (COMAGG G)

A catalogue record for this book is available from the British Library.

ISBN 0 85198 976 4

Published in association with:
Overseas Development Institute
Regent's College
Inner Circle
Regent's Park
London NW1 4NS

Printed and bound in the UK by Biddles Ltd, Guildford

Contents

Chapter 8
Conclusions 117

About the Author

Elizabeth Cromwell is an Agricultural Economist with degrees from the Universities of Reading and Oxford, specialising in the analysis of farm-level gains and losses from agricultural policies in sub-Saharan Africa. After heading the monitoring and evaluation team of a World Bank-funded agricultural project in Malawi, she has been an ODI Research Fellow since 1988. At ODI, she has participated in research assignments for the International Fund for Agricultural Development, the UN Environment Programme, the OECD, The Rockefeller Foundation and the British Overseas Development Administration. Her previous publications include:

Sowing Beyond The State: NGOs and Seed Supply in Developing Countries (with S. Wiggins and S. Wentzel) ODI, 1993.

'Malawi' in *Structural Adjustment and the African Farmer* (eds J. Howell and A. Duncan) James Currey, 1992.

'The political economy of international agricultural research: innovation for whom in the 1990s?' (book review article) *Development Policy Review*, 1993.

Agricultural Technologies for Market-Led Development: Opportunities in the 1990s (with S. Barghouti and A. Pritchard) World Bank Conference Proceedings, 1993.

Biological Diversity, Intellectual Property Rights and Plant Genetic Resources for Food and Agriculture (with D. Cooper) ODI Briefing Paper, 1993.

Preface and Acknowledgements

Over a number of years, the Overseas Development Institute's Seeds and Biodiversity Programme has researched the organisation and economics of the seed sector in developing countries. The Programme has investigated, variously, the structure of the seed sector in developing countries and how this varies from the situation in Europe and North America; the economics of the small farmer market for certified seed of modern varieties; the economic and policy factors determining small farmers' variety choices, and how these can be manipulated to promote genetically diverse agriculture; traditional community systems for seed production and exchange, and their scope and potential; and the actual and potential role of North- and South-based non-governmental organisations in seed supply to small farmers. As spin-offs from this work, the Programme has also been involved in planning and evaluating individual seed projects and programmes, investigating the economics of on-farm seed storage, assessing the impact of structural adjustment on seed supply to small farmers, and investigating the potential benefits for small farmer seed supply of manipulating seed regulatory frameworks (variety release procedures, seed certification standards, etc.).

This book draws together the results of a number of aspects of this research. The author gratefully acknowledges the financial support of the UK Overseas Development Administration and the Rockefeller Foundation for the original research. Some of the lines of argument appearing in the book represent revisions and updates of work that appeared in an OECD Development Centre *Technical Paper* (Cromwell, 1992a) and an article in *World Development* (Wiggins and Cromwell, 1995).

Thanks are due to the Governments of Malawi and Zimbabwe for permission to carry out field work, and the Zambian Department of Agricultural Research for permission to use the results of the Adaptive Research Planning Team's seed survey. The author also wishes to thank the numerous people who helped to make field work possible in the various case study countries, and who gave so generously of their time.

Elizabeth Cromwell is an Agricultural Economist and a Research Fellow at the Overseas Development Institute. She was research leader for the work on which this book is based, but for various different stages of the work she was greatly assisted by the contributions of: Esbern Friis-Hansen, Research Fellow at the Centre for Development Research, Copenhagen; Rob Tripp, formerly Assistant Director of the Economics Program of the International Maize and Wheat Improvement Center (CIMMYT), Mexico and now a Research Fellow at ODI; Michael Turner, Senior Lecturer at the Institute of Ecology and Resource Management, University of Edinburgh; Steve Wiggins, Lecturer in the Department of Agricultural Economics and Management at the University of Reading; and Batson Zambezi, formerly Head of the Government of Malawi's Chitedze Agricultural Research Station, and now with CIMMYT's Southern Africa programme.

Thanks are due to Saskia van Oosterhout for the cover photograph.

The views expressed in this book are those of the author and do not necessarily reflect those of other individuals or institutions.

Tables and Diagrams

Acronyms

ACORD	Agency for Cooperation and Research in Development
ADD	Agricultural Development Division (Malawi)
ADMARC	Agricultural Development and Marketing Corporation (Malawi)
AES	Agro-Economic Survey
AFC	Agricultural Finance Corporation (Zimbabwe)
ARDA	Agricultural and Rural Development Authority
ARPT	Adaptive Research Planning Team (Zambia)
ASA	Annual Survey of Agriculture
ASAC	Agricultural Sector Adjustment Credit
BLADD	Blantyre ADD
CDC	Commonwealth Development Corporation
CDR	Complex, Diverse and Risky Areas
CFU	Commercial Farmers' Union
CGIAR	Consultative Group for International Agricultural Research
CIAT	International Centre for Tropical Agriculture
DAR	Department of Agriculture
DR&SS	Department of Research and Specialist Services
DUS	Distinctness, Uniformity and Stability
ENDA	Environment and Development Activities – Zimbabwe
FAO	UN Food and Agriculture Organisation
FV	Farmers' Variety
GDP	Gross Domestic Product
GMB	Grain Marketing Board (Zimbabwe)
GNP	Gross National Product
GOM	Government of Malawi
GOZ	Government of Zimbabwe
GRO	Grassroots Organisation
GRZ	Government of Zambia
GTZ	Deutsche Gesellschaft für Technische Zusammenarbeit
HYV	High Yielding Varieties

IARCS	International Agricultural Research Centres
IPP	Intellectual Property Protection
KADD	Kasungu ADD
LADD	Lilongwe ADD
MCBR	Marginal Cost Benefit Ratio
MLARR	Ministry of Lands, Agriculture and Rural Resettlement (Zimbabwe)
MMD	Movement for Multi-Party Democracy
MNC	Multi-National Company
MOA	Ministry of Agriculture
MRR	Marginal Rate of Return
MV	Modern Variety
MZADD	Mzuzu ADD
NAMBOARD	National Agricultural Marketing Board
NBP	National Bean Programme
NEF	Near East Foundation
NFAZ	National Farmers' Association of Zimbabwe
NGO	Non-Governmental Organisation
NOVIB	Nederlandse Organisatie Voor Internationale Ontwikkelingssamenwerking – Dutch Organisation for International Development Co-operation
NSCM	National Seed Company of Malawi
OECD	Organisation for Economic Cooperation and Development
PCU	Provincial Co-operative Union
SACA	Smallholder Agricultural Credit Administration
SADC	Southern African Development Community
SCCI	Seed Control and Certification Institute
SIDA	Swedish International Development Aid
SSMS	Smallholder Seed Multiplication Scheme
STU	Seed Technology Unit
TC	Transactions Cost
UDI	Unilateral Declaration of Independence
UNCED	United Nations Conference on the Environment and Development
USAID	United States Agency for International Development
USC	Unitarian Service Committee
ZAMSEED	Zambia Seed Company
ZCF	Zambia Co-operative Federation
ZIMCO	Zambia Investment and Marketing Company
ZSPA	Zambia Seed Producers Association

Chapter 1

Introduction

1.1 Governments and Farmers in Africa

Within the international community there is a growing awareness of the need for a broader and deeper understanding of the relationship between governments and farmers in sub-Saharan Africa. This is in response to two trends that emerged during the 1980s: on the one hand, the widespread implementation of structural adjustment policies to liberalise agricultural markets and privatise national agricultural parastatals; and, on the other hand, the growing emphasis on development projects that involve non-governmental organisations (NGOs), as well as government staff, in the delivery of agricultural services.

During the last decade and a half, many countries in Africa have initiated programmes of structural reform in order to correct the macro-economic imbalances that developed during the 1970s and early 1980s. An important part of these programmes has been a reduction in the role of the state in economic activity in general and, given the dominance of the agricultural sector in most African economies, in agricultural produce marketing and input supply in particular. The pressure for market liberalisation was based on the belief that economic growth can best be restored by increasing competition in product and factor markets through opening them up to the private sector. However, results so far have been mixed, causing the assumptions on which this belief is based to be questioned (see for example, Commander, 1989; Mosley *et al.*, 1991). In particular, there are doubts as to whether the private sector is willing and able to fill the gap left by departing state enterprises; whether, in the absence of sufficient competition, the old state monopolies are in danger of simply being replaced by new private ones; and whether past problems with state participation in markets are more to do with the way government bureaucracies have developed than with the principle of economic regulation itself.

At the same time, there is concern that, in the short- and medium-term, the pursuit of increased macro-economic efficiency does little to solve the problems of the majority of the population. For this to happen, the agricultural stagnation of the past decade and a half must be turned round, bringing more food to the population at large and better incomes to rural dwellers. However, this cannot happen on any widespread scale until more successful efforts are made to meet the specific needs – with respect to agricultural technology and supporting agricultural services – of farmers in complex, diverse and risky environments, as it is this group who constitute the poor, rural majority throughout much of Africa.

The trend towards involving non-governmental organisations ('any organisation that is operationally distinct from government' (Farrington *et al.*, 1993)) in development projects reflects the belief that increasing local-level participation in the development process can make a positive contribution to sustainable grassroots development. This belief has arisen in part from developments in understanding of the process of innovation and change. The 'central source' model of agricultural development has been rejected and NGOs are seen as having an important role as bridging organisations, bringing together diverse actors in economic and social development (Brown, 1991). This role has been accentuated as the public sector in many developing countries withdraws from service functions, as a result of structural adjustment programmes, and other types of institution become increasingly important (Smith and Thomson, 1991).

In particular, NGOs are commonly perceived as having various advantages in working in marginal, variable environments (Farrington *et al.*, 1993). They are believed to respond to needs quickly, to be participatory – working with disadvantaged groups in disadvantaged areas – to be independent and flexible in their choice of work, information sources, communication methods and organisational structure. They are perceived as adopting an integrated approach to programmes, which includes attention to the institutional and economic context as well as to technical factors.

However, in reality the contribution of formally-organised NGOs to development needs qualification (Farrington *et al.*, 1993). In particular, they tend to focus on providing qualitative benefits, such as improved relations with local government institutions, and on encouraging client groups to explore and experiment, rather than on delivering measurable economic improvements. In income-generating projects, their emphasis on self-employment means that they tend to have problems reaching the poorest people. Furthermore, these projects are often difficult to sustain in the longer-term.

But it should be remembered that there are also a wide range of other voluntary organisations participating in the development process: alternatives to government organisations consist not just of the formally institutionalised North and South-based NGOs. In some cases, these other voluntary organisations are relatively structured membership organisations which seek to promote the welfare of members on a local scale through an agreed set of activities; in others, they are more spontaneous, loose groupings of individuals responding to an individual initiative or problem. Their involvement in the development process is likely to become increasingly important over time.

1.2 Pressures for Change in the African Seed Sector

Nowhere in the African agriculture sector are these two trends of structural adjustment and local-level participation in development gathering pace more rapidly than in the seed sub-sector. Here, the quest for alternatives to the large-scale government seed supply organisations of the 1970s and 1980s – which had only limited success in reaching the majority of farmers outside the high potential areas – is becoming more urgent in the face of Africa's stagnating crop yields and mounting food deficits. Governments and donors are recognising that these organisations, which were relatively successful in encouraging the widespread use of Green Revolution seed by Asian farmers, may not be transferable to the African context. Thus seed sector restructuring has already taken place in The Gambia, Ghana, Malawi, Mozambique, Nigeria, Tanzania and Zambia and is scheduled to happen in the near future in a number of other countries, including Côte d'Ivoire, Ethiopia and Uganda.

A third pressure for change in African seed sector organisation is concern about the appropriateness of encouraging the further use of Green Revolution seed. As we shall see in Chapter 2, there is mounting evidence that its benefits may be limited in the context of some African farming systems, whilst the international community is now recognising that the longer-term costs – in terms of loss of genetic diversity – of mono-cropping these genetically-uniform high potential yield varieties may be substantial. Genetic diversity refers both to the genes within individual plant populations and to the number of varieties of a crop; maintaining the genetic diversity of crops is necessary to enable resource-poor farmers to cope with environmental variation, to provide resistance to disease, and to protect the pool of genetic resources from which future crop varieties can be developed, amongst many other reasons.[1] In recognition of the importance of genetic diversity, an international Convention on Biological Diversity was agreed at the 1992 United Nations Conference on the Environment and Development (UNCED), committing signatories to supporting the conservation and use of a diverse range of plant genetic resources in their own domestic agriculture and globally. Clearly, changing from promoting a limited number of Green Revolution varieties to encouraging a more diverse agriculture has significant implications for how plant breeding, seed production and seed distribution are organised.

In the past, analysis of the seed sector has been neglected in Africa, compared with the attention given to other agricultural services such as produce marketing, fertiliser delivery, credit and extension. Furthermore, the analyses that have been carried out have tended to focus on the physical aspects of seed production, processing, and storage: difficulties arising from the structure and

---

[1] Good overview texts on the global value of conserving genetic diversity and the importance of genetic diversity in farming systems include McNeely *et al.*, 1990; Swanson *et al.*, 1994; Sandland and Schei, 1993; and de Boef *et al.*, 1993.

organisation of the seed sector have frequently been underestimated. Where structural and organisational issues have been touched on, it has tended to be in relation to the technical organisation of production and/or individual enterprises.[2] It is now accepted that this neglect has limited the better use of seed inputs in Africa, as problems stemming from the way the seed sector is organised are severe (DanAgro, 1987; Bentley *et al.*, 1986).

This book presents the results of the first attempt to carry out an integrated analysis of the seed sector in Africa, focusing in particular on structural and organisational aspects and the impact of the 1980s seed sector restructuring. The aim is better to understand how the relationship between governments, farmers and seeds affects performance, and thus how access to appropriate seed inputs for farmers might better be organised in the future. The book does this by applying an analytical framework to detailed case studies of Malawi, Zambia and Zimbabwe, whose seed sectors represent a range of the different structures so far tried in the sub-continent.

1.3 Seed Systems – Definitions

Before proceeding, we should explain the boundaries of this book's scope of enquiry, and define the key concepts that will be used.

The geographical focus is Africa south of the Sahara excluding South Africa: 'Africa' for short. In most African countries, small-scale, resource-poor farmers operating in complex, diverse and risky environments (Chambers, 1991) constitute a majority in terms of area cultivated and proportion of the agricultural population, and therefore form the 'client' focus for the book. We refer to this group as 'CDR farmers' or 'small farmers'.

However, the influence of other seed users on the market for seed is considered where relevant, as are the different categories of seed suppliers. With respect to seed suppliers, we make a distinction between the 'formal sector' (government, domestic and multi-national commercial companies and any other organisations that are formally constituted and involved in the supply of seeds) and the two components of the 'informal' sector: individual seed-savers, and a wide range of informal groups who share seed amongst themselves, often on an irregular basis (this latter we call the 'community seed system'). This distinction is explained in more detail in Chapter 2. The multi-national seed companies that have bought into the seed sector in a number of African countries obviously plan their activities taking into account the global trading environment. This international perspective is investigated in seed sector studies such as those by McMullen (1987), Pray and Ramaswami (1991) and Jaffee (1991); in this book, we confine our analysis to the domestic demand and supply situation operating

---

[2] The literature on seed supply in Africa is extensive. Some of the more frequently quoted studies include: Douglas, 1980; Gregg *et al.*, 1980; Kelly, 1989.

in individual countries.

As regards crops, this book deals with cereal and legume crops propagated by true seed, which are the crops of greatest importance in most complex, diverse and risky environments in Africa. Within this category, hybrid maize is a crop with its own particular characteristics in the African context so we deal with it separately (see Appendix 1). Of course, in a number of countries vegetatively-propagated crops, such as potatoes and cassava, are also very important, but they present entirely different technical seed problems and are therefore omitted from the present study. So too are the more specialised seed crops, such as vegetables and pasture grasses, as they also have quite different economic characteristics. Nonetheless, it should be recognised that such crops, especially vegetables, can play an important role in the overall marketing strategy of some seed companies and they may make a significant contribution to profits. Industrial crops, such as cotton and tobacco, are omitted because for these crops seed supply and purchase of the final crop is usually closely controlled by large processing companies which creates a very different economic environment for seed transactions.

In the past, the seed produced by formal sector seed organisations was often referred to as 'quality seed' or 'improved seed', but the implication of this – that it is better than the seed which farmers can save for themselves on-farm – is not always justified in practice. By the same token, although the formal sector is usually described as producing 'high-yielding varieties' (HYVs), these varieties do not always yield well in the complex, diverse and risky environments in which the majority of African farmers operate. The distinctions between formal sector seed and farmers' seed that do hold true are, firstly, that the former is seed of modern varieties, i.e. varieties produced using formal scientific plant breeding methods with the aim of being genetically distinct from others, and uniform and stable; and, secondly, that formal sector seed has been through a quality control process called 'seed certification', albeit sometimes imperfectly due to mechanical breakdowns, logistical problems, etc. Therefore, in this book we refer to the product of the formal sector as 'certified seed of modern varieties', or 'MV seed' for short.

Farmers' decisions to use MV seed consist of two parts. There is the initial decision to purchase MV seed for the first time. But then there is the subsequent decision to continue purchasing MV seed regularly, to avoid the deterioration in performance that occurs with certain types of MV seed if it is saved on-farm from season to season for too many years, and to enjoy the benefit of what should be clean quality-controlled seed.[3] Different factors influence these two decisions. In this book, we look at both decisions.

We call the seed that farmers save on-farm and circulate within the informal seed sector 'farmers' variety' (FV seed). This includes both landraces (material indigenous to the local area) and varieties that have had elements of exotic

---

[3] Heisey and Brennan (1991) provide a detailed examination of the factors determining the demand for this 'replacement' seed.

material incorporated, either deliberately by farmer breeders or by accident (for example, through uncontrolled cross-pollination). Farmers' varieties are much less distinct, uniform and stable than modern varieties. By definition, FV seed does not go through a formal quality control procedure in the same way as MV seed although, as we shall see in Chapter 2, farmers' own selection and handling skills can produce FV seed of very high genetic and physiological quality.

Fears of losing genetic diversity primarily relate to losing the *breadth* of the world's crop genetic resources base. However, the *control* of crop genetic resources is becoming a very important issue as a result of recent developments in the area of intellectual property protection, particularly the extension of patent-like protection to living organisms promoted in the 1993 International General Agreement on Tariffs and Trade. Discussion of control and compensation mechanisms most frequently take place at the international level: individual seed projects are not usually involved. Therefore plant patents and related issues are not a major theme in this book. However, it is important to be aware that if the current global pressure for the extension of patents is successful, increased commercial control of crop genetic resources at the international level may limit efforts to encourage diverse agriculture at local level.

1.4 How this Book is Organised

After this introductory Chapter, Chapter 2 puts the African seed sector in international and historical perspective. It starts by overviewing the development of the formal seed sector from its origins in Europe and North America. Then it contrasts the initial experience in Asia with the more recent experience in Africa and outlines the key questions that currently face seed sector organisations in Africa. Chapter 2 then identifies the different types of formal sector seed organisation, and the demand-side factors that determine the extent to which farmers in CDR areas in Africa are able and willing to use MV seed. The chapter concludes with a detailed description of the informal seed sector and why it continues to be widely used by CDR farmers in Africa.

Chapter 3 builds on this to explain how the market for MV seed works in Africa. It identifies how the formal seed sector is a framework of organisations linked together by strong longitudinal and latitudinal linkages, how five technical parameters strongly influence MV seed demand and supply, and how the market for MV seed in Africa is characterised by high transactions costs and market failure.

Chapter 4 draws together the themes presented in the previous Chapters to present a framework for seed sector analysis that can be used to assess performance at national or project level. This Chapter includes suggestions regarding data sources to use and methods of data collection. Appendix 2 gives a practical example of how this framework can be used to carry out a full-scale cost-benefit analysis for a seed project.

Chapters 5, 6 and 7 report the analyses of seed sector performance carried out in the three case study countries. Malawi provides an example of what happens when a parastatal seed company is sold to a multi-national corporation – the kind of divestment typical of many economic reform programmes in Africa. Zambia provides an example of the effect of the partial liberalisation of agricultural markets which has also been common in the region – in this case retention of the seed parastatal whilst dismantling the national network of cooperatives that served as the parastatal seed distribution system. In Zimbabwe, with its long-standing private sector seed producer cooperative, the aim was to find out whether Zimbabwe's experience provides an example of the kind of performance that might be expected in the competitive market situation that African economic reform programmes are promoting. The country chapters are particularly concerned with testing the prevailing assumptions about the relative advantages and disadvantages of different types of formal seed sector organisation.

Chapter 8 presents the study's overall conclusions concerning the relationship between governments, farmers and seeds in Africa. These conclusions cover the extent to which the organisation and structure of the seed sector determines its overall performance, the impact of the 1980s seed sector restructuring on performance, and they look beyond restructuring to the other changes that are needed in order better to meet African small farmers' seed needs. Drawing primarily on the results from the case studies in Malawi, Zambia and Zimbabwe, Chapter 8 also sets these results in context by comparing them with experience elsewhere in Africa.

For readers who are not familiar with seed production and the technical terms associated with it, Appendix 1 outlines some basic technical features of MV seed production, including generation control, self- and cross-pollination and recommended seed replacement rates.

Chapter 2

The Seed Sector in Perspective

2.1 Historical Development of the Seed Sector

For many centuries, the genetic improvement of crops depended on farmers' selection of landraces, using visual characteristics such as yield, grain size and colour. Similarly, the distribution of seed was a community-based activity, with limited diffusion occurring by means of farmer-to-farmer exchange and local trading in markets. It was not until Mendelian genetics was understood in the late nineteenth century that formal scientific plant breeding started in Europe and North America.

Formal sector plant breeding organisations have a major influence on the seed sector through their responsibility for providing new varieties. A successful plant breeding programme depends on producing varieties which show clear improvements over existing material in one or more valued attributes, without significant loss of any other important qualities. In order to keep the amount of material being screened to manageable proportions, formal sector plant breeders apply a few measurable selection criteria at an early stage in the breeding programme. Because it is not feasible to test material in all the locations where its value might be recognised, this selection strategy means that potentially useful material gets discarded. This is a fundamental dilemma in formal scientific plant breeding.

Increasing grain yield is usually the main breeding objective, with growing season length, disease resistance, the quality of the harvested product, and other agronomic attributes also taken into account. Formal sector plant breeders measure yield in terms of output per hectare, reflecting the concern of commercial farmers – the main market for MV seed in the developed world – to maximise returns per unit area. Yield trials are conducted under the high input conditions typical of commercial farms, and replicated across a wide range of agro-climatic zones. This means that breeders' trial systems tend to select the limited number of varieties able to show good yield response to inputs across a wide range of environmental conditions.

In addition, in order to facilitate control over the seed production process, modern varieties are normally expected to show a high level of genetic conformity. Thus it has become the international convention to require new varieties produced by formal sector plant breeders to meet the criteria of Distinctness, Uniformity and Stability (DUS), before permission is given for them to be released for multiplication and distribution to farmers.

Establishing a comprehensive national agricultural research system is a high cost activity, in terms of both human and financial resources, and many developing countries do not have sufficient resources to do this. Therefore, over the last 40 years, a network of international agricultural research centres (IARCs) has been established by the Consultative Group for International Agricultural Research (CGIAR) to generate material and information which can be incorporated into national agricultural research systems in developing countries relatively easily. In the context of plant breeding, which is usually the largest single activity within research programmes, the IARCs release advanced breeding lines or populations which are incorporated into national breeding programmes for further selection and/or evaluation, thus enabling formal scientific plant breeding to be used to produce modern varieties relevant to farming systems in the developing world. This system is well illustrated by the many International Rice Research Institute rice varieties which have been released over the past 25 years. Another example is the *Veery* family of wheat varieties released by the International Maize and Wheat Improvement Centre (CIMMYT) and introduced in many different developing countries.

This in turn has prompted the establishment of organised seed production and distribution in a number of developing countries, often with the support of multi- and bilateral aid projects. For example, the FAO Seed Improvement and Development Programme, which operated between 1972 and 84, provided support to 60 countries; the World Bank funded 13 national seed projects and 100 other seed-related projects during the decade to 1985; and USAID provided long-term support to the seed sector in 57 countries over a 30-year period ending in 1987. By the late 1980s sales of MV seed in developing countries accounted for 12% of global commercial seed sales, worth nearly US$4 billion annually (Groosman *et al.*, 1988).

In some parts of the developing world, especially Asia, the Green Revolution of the 1960s and 1970s was a milestone in the progress of agricultural technology: average yields of wheat and rice in Asia increased more over the 25 years to 1985 than over the whole of the previous 250 years (Lipton with Longhurst, 1989). However, the overall benefits of the Green Revolution have been hotly debated, particularly in relation to its social impact (see, for example, Farmer, 1977; Lipton with Longhurst, 1989; Conway and Barbier, 1990.

Regardless of its overall impact, the Green revolution has had an important effect on formal seed sector development in developing countries by stimulating demand for MV seed and mechanisms for distributing them. In most developing countries, no such mechanisms existed in the 1960s: the upsurge of seed sector development projects in the early 1970s was prompted by a desire on the part of governments and donors to rectify this.

In the more favoured areas of Asia where fertiliser, irrigation and farm labour are available and rice and wheat dominate, formal sector plant breeders have found it relatively easy to use their existing techniques to produce varieties with high potential yields that can be achieved in this type of farming system. Accordingly, the coverage of MV seed is now substantial in these areas and in many parts of Asia there are now numerous formal sector seed organisations, both government and private sector, providing a wide range of varieties through relatively well developed distribution systems, to various types of farmers.

In Asia the key issues in the formal seed sector are now: the social impact, because landless families and farmers without access to irrigation and too poor to afford fertiliser are not sharing in the benefits of the Green Revolution; the environmental effects of widespread high fertiliser and pesticide applications; and the likely longer-term impact of reduced genetic diversity, as a few highly stable and uniform varieties cover larger and larger areas of land. One of the most obvious immediate negative effects of this is the increased incidence of pest and disease attack. This ties farmers into regular purchase of newly-released varieties (and of chemicals), when the disease resistance of older varieties breaks down.

Comparing the area planted with MV seed in Asia and Africa (see Table 2.1), it is clear that the Green Revolution has not spread to any significant extent in Africa. This is not least because formal sector plant breeding methods are of limited application to increasing yields of the major African food crops. For the maize, millet and sorghum crops which are the major food grain crops, modern varieties cannot be produced so easily without recourse to hybridisation, and hybrid seed can be difficult for farmers in CDR areas to handle (Lipton with Longhurst, 1989). Furthermore, in large parts of Africa, farming is much more marginal: there is no irrigation, labour is in short supply and markets for fertiliser are far away (Carr, 1989). Thus, the farming system is complex, diverse and risky, so many niche varieties are required, and pest and disease resistance, drought-tolerance and a whole range of other attributes are important in addition to increasing yield. Therefore, the uptake of MV seed in these areas is low and often limited to a few crops. Less than one third of the African countries surveyed by the FAO Seed Improvement and Development Project in the mid-1980s had established formal seed production and distribution facilities for major food crops and less than 10% of total cropped area was under improved varieties (FAO, 1987). With very few exceptions, until within the last few years the majority of formal seed sector activity in Africa remained in government hands.

Thus in Africa, the key issues in the formal seed sector are now: is it appropriate to continue trying to push the uptake of conventional MV seed; or could a more eclectic approach be relevant, including, for example, greater

Table 2.1: Area planted with MV seed in Africa and Asia 1988/89 (%)

Region/Crop	Wheat	Rice	Maize
Asia			
Bangladesh	100	88	
India	86	66	
Pakistan	71	90	
Philippines		89	
Thailand	100	80	
Africa			
Ghana			30
Kenya			65
Malawi			7
Nigeria			22
Tanzania			17
Zambia			46
Zimbabwe			100

Sources: Wheat and rice = FAO, 1994
             Maize = CIMMYT, 1990

involvement of farmers in formal sector plant breeding, releasing a broader range of material, and support for informal sector seed systems. If this broader approach has potential, what are the implications for the organisation of the seed sector? In the next section, we identify the existing players in the formal seed sector and the assumed advantages and disadvantages of each type of organisation.

2.2 Types of Formal Sector Seed Suppliers

2.2.1 Public sector

These can be departments of a line ministry, such as the Ministry of Agriculture, or parastatal enterprises. For Departments, all income earned from seed sales goes straight to the Treasury and the Department is directly dependent on the government budget for funds; parastatals have more financial autonomy, although their operational strategies are still strongly influenced by government policy rather than by the market situation alone. Public sector seed organisations have historically dominated the formal seed sector in Africa.

Profit-making is not usually the primary objective of this type of seed organisation, although importance may be attached to cost-recovery. Serving all types of farmer, and particularly those less able to participate in commercial seed markets, can be an important part of the mandate of public sector seed organisations. This can oblige them to deal in a wide range of seeds, including those that are relatively high cost to produce (for example, groundnuts) and/or relatively low value (beans, rice, etc.). It also means that they have a harder task to perform in delivering seed in good time for planting, because timely delivery is harder in the more remote areas without good roads.

The degree of government control and investment in public sector seed organisations varies between countries, and may change over time in response to changes in economic policy and external pressures. Policy often has a significant influence on seed pricing. Furthermore, cumbersome bureaucratic procedures, for example for the allocation of vehicles, can make it hard for public sector seed organisations to perform well.

Often, such organisations have great difficulty in meeting either cost recovery or service delivery objectives. The experiences in the 1980s of the Seed Multiplication Unit of the Department of Agriculture in The Gambia and of the Tanzania Seed Company are typical: the former recorded a turnover of less than 10% of its US$89,600 expenditure in 1984/85, at the same time as having 'a very limited impact on the national seed supply position' according to one evaluation (Republic of The Gambia, 1987); the latter made losses of around US$580,000 in 1982/83 in the process of supplying less than 14% of Tanzania's estimated seed requirements (Budden, 1986).

2.2.2 Private sector

These include both multi-national companies (MNCs), such as Pioneer and Cargill, and indigenous small- and medium-scale seed enterprises. In the past, this type of seed organisation has not had a large presence in the African seed sector, but their presence is now growing following the 1980s restructurings.

Profitability is an important objective for private sector seed organisations. This dictates a market-oriented operational strategy geared to providing those types of seed for which there is effective demand (usually varieties which have to be replaced every season and are popular with commercial farmers) and which are profitable to produce (those with high multiplication factors and controlled breeding systems (for example, hybrids) are usually the most profitable). Furthermore, for cost reasons most private sector seed companies deal in only a limited number of varieties and seed is sold in standard pack sizes (typically sufficient to plant one hectare at recommended sowing rates). Private sector activities are normally carefully targeted to specific types of farmers or crops and will swiftly change orientation if that particular sales area becomes less profitable.

Both public and private sector seed organisations sometimes decentralise seed multiplication to the local level, by recruiting farmers as contract seed growers. However, operational control is retained by the seed organisation.

2.2.3 Voluntary organisations

These include the more formally-organised NGOs, originating in Europe/North America and the developing world, and a broad range of more informal grass-roots organisations, such as member cooperatives, community organisations and church groups. Some North-based NGOs are involved in seed activities on their own account, whilst others provide funding and other support to grassroots organisations. In many African countries, economic activity was dominated by the public sector until the mid-1980s, and voluntary organisations were not tolerated, except in the provision of relief aid in emergencies and for the destitute. It is only since economic liberalisation that the role of voluntary organisations in development has increased and diversified.

Voluntary organisations usually become involved in the seed sector for developmental reasons rather than to generate income. They can substitute for, complement or create an alternative to public and private sector seed activities, depending on the situation. As far as formal NGOs are concerned, in addition to their traditional role of providing relief seed distribution after emergencies, they may be seeking to act as a substitute source of supply of MV seed to farmers who are unserved by other types of seed organisation because they are poor or remote, or because the government system is not operating effectively. Or some voluntary organisations may be trying to empower communities by helping them to multiply FV seed and landraces locally and thus to conserve genetic diversity at the local level. This is becoming increasingly popular with many south-based NGOs. By definition, it is antagonistic to the spread of MV seed but some voluntary organisations consider such a strategy to be important for the sustainability of traditional small farm farming systems, given the increased dependency and risk that the use of MV seed can involve. Or voluntary organisations may be acting as advocates for disadvantaged groups, by lobbying on their behalf nationally or internationally and providing information and analytical support. Strengthening farmers' rights to plant genetic resources has been a particular focus in this area.

Clearly voluntary organisations span the divide between the formal and informal seed sectors. Some formal NGOs control all activities and resources and effectively act as an intermediary in the production and distribution chain of the formal seed sector. For other voluntary organisations seed activities originate in a desire to help communities be more self-sufficient, in which case farmers themselves may control activities and these activities may be relatively unstructured and have FV seed as the focus of operations. Despite this diversity, two general observations about voluntary organisation seed activities can be made: first, it is much more common for voluntary organisations to set up new structures for seed multiplication and distribution than to build on existing structures within communities; second, many voluntary organisations have relatively little understanding of the genetic and physiological attributes of the seed they work with (Cromwell *et al.*, 1993).

Despite all the activity of public, private and voluntary seed organisations, the seed they produce represents no more than 20% of the total amount planted in both developed and developing countries. Even seed companies and government agricultural extension services, which tend to be over-optimistic about potential seed sales, rarely assume farmers will buy seed more frequently than once in four years, as this would be an unnecessary expense. Thus the informal sector remains very important worldwide. We will examine the characteristics of the informal seed sector in Africa later in this Chapter. To help to understand *why* it is important, however, it will be helpful if we first look at the different types of farmers who buy seed in Africa, their objectives in doing so and the resources available to them to purchase seed.

2.3 Types of Farmer Seed-Purchasers

2.3.1 Commercial farmers

Commercial farmers are mostly located in relatively high potential areas with well-established market infrastructure. Their main operational objective is to maximise marketable surpluses. The purchase of MV seed is an important means of achieving this; it also offers managerial convenience and flexibility (avoiding the need to allocate scarce resources to producing or storing farm-saved seed; and to be tied to using a limited number of varieties).

Although numerically the smallest category of seed user in Africa, commercial farmers' buying power is strong so this group has historically exerted a strong influence on the directions pursued by formal sector plant breeders and on the way the formal seed sector has developed. For example, for many years the main emphasis in maize breeding in Kenya and in Zimbabwe was on producing the hybrids useful to commercial farmers (Rusike, 1995), rather than the open-pollinated varieties which are a more realistic option for farmers in CDR areas who find it expensive and difficult to replace seed every year and who do not have the resources to exploit the potential of hybrid varieties.

2.3.2 Subsistence farmers

Few purely subsistence farmers remain in Africa, because the level of market penetration means most farmers are now integrated into the commercial economy for at least some consumption goods, and therefore for a proportion of production activities. Most subsistence farmers have to save their own seed on-farm or rely on the relatives and neighbours for their seed needs. Until their wider resource constraints are addressed, so that they are able to participate more fully in conventional markets, supplying subsistence farmers through the formal seed sector is unlikely to be feasible – although there may be an important role for NGOs that can work to alleviate this group's resource constraints at the same time as making seed available.

2.3.3 Farmers in complex, diverse and risky areas

Farm households' attitude towards agricultural innovations, of which MV seed is an example, is determined by relative factor scarcities, household production objectives, and resource allocation mechanisms in the wider economy. Here, we consider these variables for farmers in CDR areas, who are the focus of this book.

These farmers are operating areas of comparatively low agricultural potential, with less fertile soils and lower and more variable rainfall. Also, they are typically relatively remote from market centres, with no ready market for surplus production, nor easy access to external farm inputs. According to farmers interviewed in a range of adoption studies covering different crops and countries in Africa surveyed by Lawrence (1988), this is a strong disincentive to using modern varieties as the effectiveness of back-up services such as input supply, credit, extension advice and product marketing is the single most important influence on farmers' decisions to use MVs, given their suitability to the farming system. Neither is this latter assured as, historically, these areas have received less attention from formal sector agricultural research, as have the crops grown in them, because the potential returns to research are lower in these areas and because, as we saw earlier in this Chapter, it is difficult to produce results for them using formal sector agricultural research methods.[4, 5]

CDR households often have limited land; usually they have access to large areas in absolute terms only where the land is of low potential. This is partly because in many African countries, population densities are now reaching high levels, and partly because of the basis for allocating rights to land. With respect to the latter, in many countries farm families obtain rights under customary tenure only to the area of land that they can regularly cultivate. With access only to hand tools and with widespread migration of male family members to urban employment, this area is often relatively small. Further pressure on land exists in those countries which have not altered the concentration of the small farm population into relatively small areas that arose from the allocation of large parts of the most fertile areas to large-scale commercial farmers during colonial times.

They usually have limited capital resources too: much farm production does not enter monetised market systems and what cash there is from crop sales has to be used for other household needs; for various reasons to do with poor access and high real interest rates, they do not use formal or informal credit either.

Thus, the only resource over which these households have some control is labour. But this, too, may be in short supply for on-farm agricultural production:

---

[4] References exploring African farming systems in more detail include Low, 1986; Ali and Byerlee, 1991; Carr, 1989; and Collinson, 1989.

[5] For further information on the problems of agricultural research for CDR farmers, see Arndt *et al.*, 1977; Ahmed and Ruttan, 1988; Arnon, 1989; Lipton with Longhurst, 1989; or Kaimowitz, 1990.

in many parts of Africa, there is often a higher return to the household's most productive labour resources (mobile, adult males) in local off-farm employment or as migrant labour. The women who are left behind, who throughout Africa do the bulk of the physical work involved in food crop production, face conflicting demands on their time from domestic chores, such as water and fuelwood collection, child care and food preparation. Coupled with low producer prices and subsidised food, this has meant that in many countries it has been more sensible to allocate productive labour off-farm and to buy in food when necessary. Thus in these circumstances, where returns are measured per unit of labour time rather than per unit of land, incorporating labour-intensive modern varieties into the farming system is not feasible or economically rational. The evidence available so far suggests that the contraction in off-farm employment brought about by the 1980s recession and structural adjustment has not produced a return of migrants to the farming sector: rather, they prefer to remain in urban areas, piecing work together in the informal sector.

As a result of these factor constraints, the agricultural production system of farm households in CDR areas is geared primarily to meeting domestic consumption needs for food and other natural resource products (roofing and fencing materials, animal fodder, etc.), whilst minimising production risk. However, the production system typically includes some commercially-oriented activities, and some commercial transactions take place as a by-product of food production activities (sale of food crops in surplus years, beer-brewing, etc.).

2.4 The Seed Needs of Farmers in CDR Areas

The characteristics of the farming system in CDR areas mean that farmers in these areas have a particular set of seed needs, compared with other seed users.

2.4.1 Crop varieties

In CDR areas, households want seed for a large number of different crops. They also want seed of numerous different varieties for each crop, to allow for, firstly, the varied physical environments in which they plant each crop (valley bottom and hill-side; different soil types; interplanted, stagger planted and pure stand; main season and off-season, etc.) and, secondly, the numerous end uses of each crop (human consumption of the grain, leaves and roots; beer-brewing; straw and stovers for animal fodder, roofing and fencing; storage as an emergency food stock; selling for cash). Thirdly, different varieties (early-maturing, late-maturing, able to withstand dry spells) are required to enable farm households to cope with the riskiness of seasons in CDR areas without the use of external inputs. Material with a high degree of genetic variation can be very important for this purpose.

Thus most households will grow a large number of varieties of each crop. For beans, for example, a recent survey in Malawi found more than 35 phenotypically different types in farmers' mixtures (Ferguson, 1992). Other surveys provide similar results: in Ethiopia, households were found to be growing at least four varieties of their main crop (Singh, 1990); in Zimbabwe, more than 10 varieties of sorghum were in common use in three areas surveyed by van Oosterhout (1992); and in Sierra Leone, 60 distinct rice varieties were found in one village, with each household growing 4–8 varieties (Richards, 1985).

As well as yielding without large applications of external inputs, other attributes are important. These can include, depending on the crop and the situation: low labour requirements; pest and disease resistance; particular processing, cooking and taste qualities; storability; and good yield of non-grain biomass (leaves, stalks, etc.).

There can be an important role for MV seed in certain circumstances. These include where environmental change is forcing households to modify traditional farming systems: the use of early-maturing MVs can be a valuable method for coping with declining rainfall, for example. In The Gambia, the short duration modern variety of rice, *Peking*, has almost completely replaced local cultivars in North Bank Division (Cromwell *et al.*, 1993), whilst in Malawi the early-maturing maize hybrids *NSCM 41* and *MH18* are widely used as part of households' variety portfolios to reduce the risk of crop failure from short rains (Smale, pers. comm.). But it is difficult to provide many of the other variety attributes preferred by CDR farmers using formal sector plant breeding methods.

Thus, instead, it is often material maintained within the community that is most suited to CDR farmers' needs. These can be landraces, such as the high lysine sorghum *MarChuke* found in Wello, Ethiopia (Gebrekidan and Kebede, 1979). However, there are few true landraces left in use in most areas. Or they can be farmer varieties (FVs). These can take various forms. They can be selections from landraces made by farm households on the basis of visible characteristics such as plant height and architecture, grain size and colour. An example of this is the *Gbengben* medium-duration rice variety that has been developed from local cultivars by farmers in the scarp foot zone of Sierra Leone (Richards, 1985). Or they can be exotic material which has been maintained on-farm and incorporated into the farming system. Examples include seed brought back by travellers and grains saved from distributions of food aid. In East Africa, the maize varieties *Asikari* and *KAR* (from 'Kings African Rifles') are examples of this latter, having been maintained by farm households from the seed handed out to soldiers on their demobilisation at the end of World War II (Friis-Hansen, 1988). The sorghum cultivar *Reagen*, now widely grown in Western Sudan, is an example of the former, having been saved from food aid distributed during the 1984 drought (Croxton, pers. comm.).

Past releases by formal sector plant breeders form another category and indicate the latent demand for new varieties in CDR areas (ARPT, 1991; Smale, pers. comm.). There are many examples of this, including the *Bingo* maize variety in common use in many areas in Malawi, which is derived from the 1960s' *LH11* maize release, and the *Mutengu* sorghum variety used in Eastern

Kenya, which is derived from past releases of *Serena* sorghum (Nyongesa and Johnson, 1990).

2.4.2 Seed quantities

For seed stocks maintained on-farm, households will generally aim to save sufficient seed to last two seasons in order to allow for the risk of complete harvest failure or the need to replant. But when sourcing seed off-farm only small quantities of each variety are required, because each household grows many different varieties and often plants at lower than recommended densities and replaces seed less frequently than recommended by professional seed technologists.[6] For example, in Malawi 75% of households growing soyabeans, and over 40% of households growing beans, replace seed less frequently than every five years.

Thus surveys in Zambia and Burundi respectively indicate that households typically seek to acquire no more than 10kg of maize seed and 15kg of bean seed per cropping season (ARPT, 1991; Sperling, 1993). Our own survey carried out in Malawi reports typical quantities as being 5kg for maize, 14kg for groundnuts and 6kg for beans.

2.4.3 Seed quality

Households in CDR areas do not want nor need seed to meet all the standards that formal sector variety release and seed certification systems provide. Whilst the physical purity of seed and reasonable germination percentages are valued (Delouche, 1982, suggests 70% rather than the 95% required for formal sector seed certification), uniform seed size and varieties' conformity to DUS criteria are often irrelevant.

At the same time, households are unwilling to pay for the additional cost of packed seed (packing seed is an integral component of formal sector seed certification schemes) and, as we will see in the country studies in subsequent Chapters, standard packs are in any case often split up between relatives and neighbours because they are too big. Households will happily use seed from crops they have seen growing on neighbours' land, substituting 'neighbour certification' for formal seed certification (Singh, 1990), which is not visible, and anyway often does not guarantee seed quality where seed is stored in poor conditions after leaving the processing plant.

---

[6] For a discussion of the factors determining farmers' demand for replacement seed, see Heisey and Brennan, 1991.

2.4.4 Access to seed

Availability of seed in good time for planting is critical for farm households in CDR areas for two reasons: first, because delayed planting has a much greater impact on eventual yield in these areas than in higher potential areas (Edwards *et al.*, 1988; Low and Waddington, 1990); second, because farm households in CDR areas cannot afford to tie up cash in buying stocks of seed to hold in advance of the planting season.

As regards accessibility of seed distribution points, households will travel a long way to source seed if they are convinced of its superiority to their own stocks. However, they dislike doing this and nearness of supply is commonly mentioned as a plus factor for the informal seed sector that outweighs some of the disadvantages of using this source of seed (ARPT, 1991; Sperling, 1993). Results from Zambia, for example, indicate the average distance travelled to source seed as being 2–6km (Muliokela and Mwale, pers. comm.).

2.4.5 Agronomic advice

Farmers in CDR areas can be extremely adept at maintaining FVs on-farm and using them to best effect, as we will see later in this Chapter. The methods and timing for planting, cultivating, storing the harvest and selecting seed for FVs have been fine-tuned over the years in each local area. Families pass this information on to new generations: in many cultures in Africa, not only a stock of seed but also advice about how best to use it is automatically provided to each new family unit as they set up their household.

However, many MVs represent a completely new production technology for farmers in CDR areas (Gerhart, 1975; Edwards *et al.,* 1988). This is not only in terms of the complementary inputs needed to maximise yield, but also in terms of the timing of planting, methods of cultivation, and all the other husbandry techniques involved in crop production. It applies to crops farmers are already growing, using FV seed, as much as to new crops being introduced into the farming system. As we will see in the country case studies in later chapters, there is much evidence which shows that, if the new management techniques are not adopted, the benefit from using MV seed will be minimal.

Therefore, whilst communities' indigenous knowledge is both sufficient and essential for the cultivation of FV seed, additional sources of agronomic advice are needed when MV seed is introduced. This can take many forms: direct contract with government agricultural extension agents or seed companies' sales representatives, radio programmes, leaflets distributed with packs of seed, etc. There is evidence from Asia, where MV seed has been in use longer than in Africa, that farmers themselves are often an important source of advice. For example, Heisey (1990) and Green (1985) report that in Pakistan and Nepal respectively the first farmers to use MV seed often become the main source of agronomic advice for later adopters.

2.5 Seed Sources Used by Farmers in CDR Areas

Bearing in mind relative factor scarcities and their household production objectives, there are four main options for sourcing seed open to farm households in CDR areas:

1. to maintain seed on-farm;
2. to supplement on-farm stocks with seed from off-farm sources;
3. to buy in all seed fresh each season;
4. to seek altogether new varieties from off-farm sources.

The decisions reached vary significantly between households at different stages in the family life cycle and with different resource endowments. This is because the farming system of households in CDR areas has to be highly diverse and also dynamic: constantly changing in response to changes in the family life cycle and in external conditions (climatic variation, off-farm wage rates, crop prices, agricultural innovations, etc.). All this results in complex patterns of seed sourcing (and individual households will use different sources of seed over time) but, broadly-speaking, at any given point in time three different categories of households can be distinguished:

seed secure households (usually the better-resourced households), who save the majority of seed needed on-farm but may use off-farm sources in order to experiment with new varieties;

crisis-prone households who are seed-secure in most seasons but are less well-resourced, so a domestic crisis, such as harvest failure or death or illness in the family, can force them to augment saved seed with off-farm supplies;

chronically insecure households who are poorly resourced and so in most seasons are unable to harvest sufficient crops to meet seed and domestic consumption needs.

Increased use of MV seed may have significant potential for increasing output per unit area but, as we saw above, this may not be an important objective for farmers in CDR areas. Furthermore, their ability to make use of formal sector seed organisations is constrained by the difficult physical and economic environment in which they operate. Thus, some 60–70% of seed used by CDR farmers in Africa is saved on-farm.[7] Of the remainder, MV seed constitutes at most a further 10%. The remaining 30–40% or more is sourced from relatives,

---

[7] For detailed estimates see, for example, Dougnac and Kokwe, 1988; Friis-Hansen, 1988; Nyongesa and Johnson, 1990; ARPT, 1991.

neighbours and other community sources. In Ethiopia, for example, a recent seed survey found that between 25% and 50% of farm households borrow or buy seeds every year but most transactions take place between neighbours and relatives (Singh, 1990). In Malawi, as we shall see in Chapter 5, two thirds of all bean seed used is obtained from neighbours, relatives and other local sources. This community seed system is particularly important to chronically insecure and crisis-prone households, but it is also used by seed secure households, because of the difficulties in sourcing seed from the formal sector in CDR areas, and the inappropriateness of many of the MVs supplied. In the Great Lakes region of East Africa, for example, it has been found that although 40% of farmers obtain some bean seed off-farm, as few as 10% do so to obtain modern varieties (Sperling, 1993).

2.6 The Informal Seed Sector

The informal sector includes all the methods, apart from buying seed from formal sector organisations, by which farmers can obtain their seed requirements. These methods fall into two sub-groups: retaining seed on-farm from previous harvests which, as we saw above, is the most common means of sourcing seed for CDR farmers in Africa; and the community seed system – i.e. farmer-to-farmer seed exchange based on barter, social obligation, etc. – which is the next most important source of seed for CDR farmers.

The reason for CDR farmers' reliance on community seed systems rather than the formal seed sector is that these systems have five key characteristics which give them a clear advantage in serving this group of farmers:

1. they use existing **indigenous structures** for information flow and exchange of goods: these are not necessarily static over time in the way they operate, but they are well established and well understood within the community;
2. they are **informal** in the way that they operate, changing over time and not subject to the same rigidities of organisation and operation as formal sector organisations. Farmers can participate in them as and when they want;
3. they operate mainly at the **community level**, between households within a small number of communities, although lines of supply may extend over a relatively wide geographical area. So farmers do not have to travel far to source seed;
4. a wide variety of **exchange mechanisms** are used to transfer seed between individuals and households, not just cash sales but also in-kind seed loans, barter and transfers based on social obligations. This is an important means of giving a wide range of socio-economic groups access to seed, because in many areas cash purchases and transactions using formal sector credit are limited to the better-resourced households (Smale, pers. comm.). The need to pay cash is cited frequently as a disincentive to the use of formal sector seed (Friis-Hansen, 1988;

ARPT, 1991; Muliokela and Mwale, pers. comm.);

5. the individual **quantities** of seed exchanged are often very small compared with the amounts formal sector organisations typically deal in.

There has been little research into the social equity, or otherwise, of community seed systems. The limited work that has been done suggests that this is influenced by the existing degree of social differentiation within communities, and the nature of patron–client relations, and in some communities may be more discriminatory than so far assumed (Cromwell, 1990; Sperling, 1993). For example, access to seed may be limited to certain ethnic or social groups; or access mechanisms may perpetuate poverty through requiring large quantities of seed to be returned in payment for in-kind seed loans.

In no part of Africa is there any evidence that individual farmers or communities set themselves up permanently as seed producers. Rather, individuals, who may change from year to year, are approached by other members of the community because they are seen to have a good stand of crops growing or they have planted a new variety which appears to be performing well. The exception to this is where individuals with some kind of traditional status (village headmen, large landowners, etc.) are approached by poorer households in patterns of traditional obligations of patronage.

In the formal sector seed technology literature, it is taken as given that formal scientific plant breeding and quality control result in better quality seed, genetically and physiologically, than what can be produced within the community.

However, there is now an increasing amount of work being done to test this assumption and, as we shall see in the following sections, it appears that it is not always valid. The typical farmer seed production process is outlined in Box 2.1.

2.6.1 Farmer plant breeding

Community seed systems have a clear advantage in meeting CDR farmers' variety needs as these systems deal with a large number of farmer varieties as well as adaptations of MVs.

The old belief that the risk-aversity of CDR farmers means they do not experiment (Shapiro, 1977) is not borne out in practice: many farmers in CDR areas pursue the economically logical strategy of coping with risk by conducting small-scale experiments with a wide variety of planting material. Carefully documented variety performance records have been found in a number of farming communities (for example, in Ethiopia as described by Mooney in Cooper *et al.*, 1992).

Farmer breeders use not only landraces and modern varieties from the formal sector, but also varieties that they have developed themselves. Before scientific plant breeding began, the genetic improvement of crops depended entirely on farmers' selection from local material, using visual characteristics: thus, farmers have for many centuries been actively involved in plant breeding and breeding skills within many community seed systems are highly developed.

Box 2.1: Farmer-managed seed production process

- **Growing**: many farmers rogue their growing crops by hand to remove diseased plants, and remove off-type plants as well. Farmers usually do mass selection on basis of visual appearance of individual grains rather than plants. This is usually, although not always, done in-field pre-harvest.

- **Harvest**: crops are harvested by hand so mechanical damage to the seed and contamination with seeds and other inert material are avoided.

- **Cleaning**: after harvest, crops are often threshed and cleaned by hand, again limiting damage and contamination.

- **Drying**: crops are usually dried in the sun, which can reduce moisture content to satisfactory levels – although there is some danger of scorching and killing seeds if the crop is left in the direct sun for long periods.

- **Storage**: considerable care is often taken in the storage of seeds: local insecticides and fungicides (for example, eucalyptus leaves, sand, ash, neem) can be added to the crop, which is then placed in special sealed containers which are themselves stored in places, such as above the fireplace, best suited to keeping the seed pest- and disease-free and viable. In damp climates, seed is often removed from store and re-dried a number of times during the course of the storage period.

- **Conditioning**: it is less common for small farmers to do any kind of germination testing prior to planting the stored seed and there is no documentation of any traditional pre-germination seed treatments being applied. However, in certain areas, where the incidence of pre-germination pest and fungus attack is high, and modern chemical seed treatments are available cheaply (for example, in Eastern Kenya, parts of Mali and parts of Eastern Sudan), these are now widely used on saved seed.

Source: Delouche in CIAT, 1982.

The most straightforward farmer plant breeding technique is mass selection, but there is evidence that farmers can also carry out controlled crossing successfully (Montecinos and Altieri in Cooper *et al.*, 1992). The Africa Seeds of Survival project in Ethiopia estimates that yield increases of 3.5% per year can be obtained from on-farm selection from farmer varieties of crops such as teff, sorghum and millet (USC, 1988). Also, there are a number of other documented examples of farmers' success in variety maintenance and development. For example, the community-controlled seed selection and maintenance practised in Tigray, Eritrea meant that, when seed banks were established in response to the droughts and wars of the late 1980s, it was found – contrary to expectations – that farmers had finely-tuned seed selection skills which allowed them to maintain a large diversity of varieties of different crops, including small-seeded ones such as teff and millet (Berg, 1992).

Where farmers find it difficult to select varieties for certain attributes, they often develop alternative techniques for dealing with the problem. A good example of this is the technique of planting mixes of large numbers of individual bean varieties in single plots, which has been well documented in East Africa. This technique allows farmers to overcome the difficulty of selecting individual bean varieties with resistance to the wide range of prevalent pests and diseases; instead, they can be sure that, whatever combination of pests or diseases attacks their crop in any one season, there will be a sufficient proportion of plants resistant to that combination. The value of this technique is being recognised by some formal sector bean breeders and seed producers. Instead of trying to produce bean varieties to replace traditional mixes, breeders are now aiming to produce varieties that can be incorporated into existing mixes. This new approach is well documented in, for example, the reports of the Collaborative Research Support Project in Malawi (MSU, 1987).

2.6.2 On-farm seed conditioning and storage

Once seed has been harvested, its quality can be maintained but not improved. Practices used in the conditioning and storage of seed will directly affect quality maintenance, as the environment in which seed is kept influences quality more than the actual age of the seed (Barton, 1961).

In many CDR areas in Africa, high temperature and/or relative humidity make it particularly difficult to condition and store seed on-farm successfully. Nonetheless, the limited evidence that has been collected – by, for example, CIAT in the Great Lakes region of East Africa and by Wright *et al.* (1994) for Africa as a whole – suggests that there is a considerable amount of indigenous technical knowledge within farming communities about solutions to on-farm storage problems using locally-available materials. Seed may be stored separately from grain, in which case it is commonly hung on the head in a smoky place such as the kitchen, to minimise insect damage and reduce the moisture content (Mpande, 1992; Tyler, pers. comm.). Where seed is stored in containers, it is sometimes mixed with a natural insecticide, such as neem or an inert filler, such as ash or sand. However, often no distinction is made between the seed and food grain parts of a crop until planting time, and they are conditioned and stored together.

2.6.3 Quality of farm-saved seed

Farmers' indigenous seed care skills and technologies appear consistently to produce seed of equal or better quality than formal sector seed at the point of sale. They may indeed have an inherent advantage in doing so, because it is much easier to carry out the special procedures required when the quantities are small. For example, the CIAT Great Lakes Regional Programme in East Africa recently conducted experiments to measure the comparative quality of bean seed saved by farmers and seed obtained from the local agricultural research station and found 'no statistical differences . . . in terms of vigour, emergence and yield' (CIAT, 1992:4).

Except in certain environments where seed-borne diseases or off-season storage is a particular problem, the physical quality of seed sourced from community seed systems is usually adequate. Gore (1987) reports that trials for farmer varieties collected in Zimbabwe show germination percentages of above 94% for maize and 'higher than expected' for sorghum and millet.

Genetic quality is also usually adequate, because a considerable amount of in-field roguing of off-types and post-harvest selection takes place (in any case, most households prefer to have some intra-varietal variation in the seed that they plant). The On-Farm Seed Production Project which operates in Senegal and The Gambia found that, for self-pollinated crops like rice, varietal purity of farm-saved seed is high (Osborn, 1990). Although this is obviously higher for cross-pollinated crops, Heisey and Brennan (1991) report average yield losses from own-saved seed of self-pollinated crops of just 0.75% per cropping season.

Chapter 3

The Market for Modern Variety Seed

3.1 Producers and Consumers

The formal seed sector can be defined as a framework of organisations linked together by their involvement in or influence on the multiplication, processing and distribution of MV seed (Walker, 1980). These organisations include not only those directly involved in the formally organised multiplication, processing, distribution and quality control of MV seed but a range of linked organisations and structures at national and community level that exert an important influence on the seed market. Diagram 3.1 shows the components of the formal seed sector and the linkages between them.

Two key characteristics may be distinguished: longitudinally, from plant breeding to eventual uptake by farmers, MV seed production proceeds through a sequence of linked operations which form a chain. At the same time, successful MV seed supply depends on strong latitudinal linkages to other agricultural services which collectively form a package. The success of any one component of the formal seed sector is thus strongly influenced by the performance of the other components and by the strength of the linkages between them: the sector as a whole is only as successful as its weakest link. Furthermore, different types of organisations are often responsible for separate parts of the seed chain and package: some parts are intrinsically more susceptible to private sector involvement (e.g. marketing MV seed to commercial farmers) than others (e.g. quality control, supplying seed to farmers in CDR areas).

Having strong linkages between organisations is an important requirement in the formal seed sector, and all decisions made by producers and consumers have to take adequate account of them. It is vital for seed producers that they can rely on punctual inspection of seed crops by the seed quality control services; and it is equally vital for farmers intending to buy MV seed from the formal sector that they can get sufficient fertiliser for planting this kind of seed to be worthwhile.

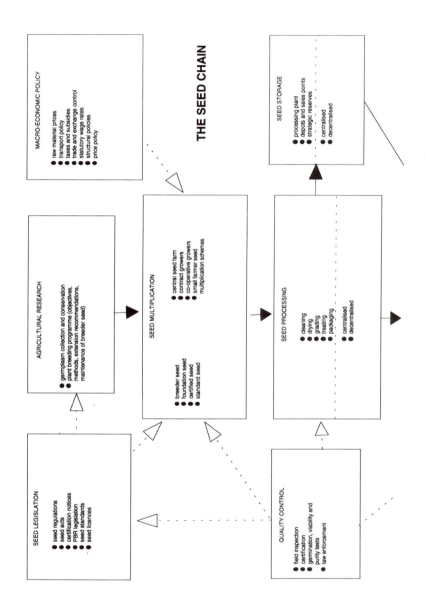

THE SEED CHAIN

MACRO-ECONOMIC POLICY
- raw material prices
- transport policy
- taxes and subsidies
- trade and exchange control
- statutory wage rates
- structural policies
- price policy

AGRICULTURAL RESEARCH
- germplasm collection and conservation
- plant breeding programme (objectives, methods, extension recommendations, maintenance of breeder seed)

SEED LEGISLATION
- seed regulations
- seed acts
- certification notices
- PBR legislation
- seed standards
- seed licences

SEED MULTIPLICATION
- breeder seed
- foundation seed
- certified seed
- standard seed

- central seed farm
- contract growers
- co-operative growers
- small farmer seed multiplication schemes

SEED PROCESSING
- cleaning
- drying
- grading
- treating
- packaging

- centralised
- decentralised

QUALITY CONTROL
- field inspection
- certification
- germination, viability and purity tests
- law enforcement

SEED STORAGE
- processing plant
- depots and sales points
- strategic reserves

- centralised
- decentralised

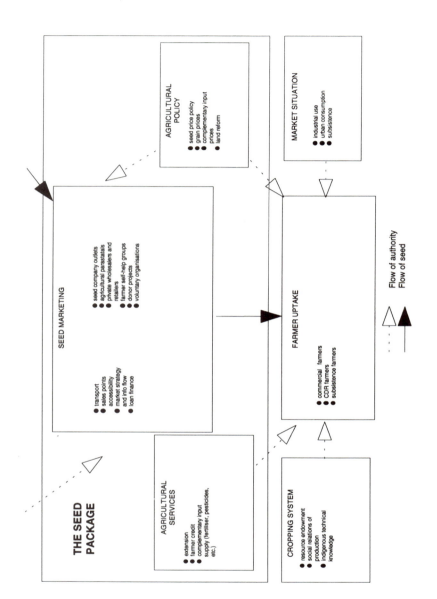

Diagram 3.1: The seed sector – organisational framework

3.2 The Product

Five technical parameters for MV seed production and use[8] determine farmers' attitudes towards using MV seed and seed organisations' attitudes towards producing MV seed. Table 3.1 summarises the ways in which the objectives of formal sector seed organisations and CDR farmers differ with regard to these parameters.

The first point to emphasise is that each side weights the five parameters differently. Taking CDR farmers first, a difficult environment for producing or storing seed on-farm is one of the major factors pushing them to source seed off-farm, as is growing crops with a breeding system (such as cross-pollination) which is difficult to manage on-farm. In the African context, these two factors push CDR farmers towards sourcing seed off-farm for crops such as beans, soyabeans, and hybrid crops (in Africa, this latter means primarily hybrid maize).

However, after this first stage in the farmer decision process, the environmental adaptability of available varieties starts to exert an influence: where the available MV seed is not well adapted to performing in complex, diverse, and risky environments – as is the case with many modern varieties – farmers will tend to seek alternative sources who can provide varieties better adapted to the environment – usually within the community seed system. For crops where the MV seed available from formal sector seed organisations does pass the test of performing under CDR conditions, a third set of factors determines farmers' ultimate purchasing decisions: for cost reasons, farmers in CDR areas will be more attracted towards using MV seed for those crops with low sowing rates (such as maize) and slow rates of deterioration (such as beans).

Formal sector seed organisations see the parameters rather differently. With a view to maximising returns, the breeding system and rate of deterioration are the two most influential factors: suppliers are most interested in producing MV seed for self-pollinated crops (such as rice, wheat, and legumes) or controlled cross-pollinated crops (such as maize), because for these crops they can manage the seed production process successfully (the latter has the added advantage that most farmers in CDR areas cannot manage it successfully themselves because of the need to isolate crops grown for seed); and they also seek out crops with high rates of deterioration (such as hybrid maize) – both in the interests of guaranteeing regular seed sales. After this primary selection, suppliers then seek to minimise production costs by choosing those crops with high multiplication factors (maize again) and those modern varieties with wide environmental adaptability. A final consideration is the production and storage environment: usually this can be controlled by, for example, irrigation, isolation and temperature- and humidity-controlled storage; only in exceptional circumstances will this factor prove to have a fundamental influence on suppliers' decisions about what kinds of seed to produce.

---

[8] Explained in Appendix 1.

Table 3.1: Technical parameters encouraging MV seed use and seed production

		Small Farmer Seed User	*Commercial Seed Supplier*
Breeding system	Parameter	Cross-pollinated	Self-pollinated or controlled cross-pollinated
	Suitable crop/variety	Hybrid maize	Rice, wheat, legumes, hybrid maize
Multiplication factor/ sowing rate	Parameter	Low sowing rate	High multiplication factor
	Suitable crop/variety	Maize, sorghum, millet	Maize, sorghum, millet
Rate of deterioration/ frequency of purchase	Parameter	Low	High
	Suitable crop/variety	Wheat, rice, beans, groundnuts	Hybrid maize
Environmental adaptability	Parameter	Location-specific	Wide
	Suitable crop/variety	Farmers' varieties	Modern varieties
Production/storage environment	Parameter	Difficult	Favourable or controllable
	Suitable crop/variety	Beans, soyabeans	Most crops

Note: See Appendix 1 for explanation of technical terms

Thus, not only do formal sector seed organisations and farmers in CDR areas give different weight to the various technical parameters, but also, for each one, they have significantly different objectives. Taken altogether, it is clear that in general there are few crops and modern varieties in which the interests of formal sector seed organisations and farmers in CDR areas coincide, the main example in the African context being hybrid maize. The particular case of hybrid maize

Type of seed / Seed system	Farmers' varieties	Enhanced FVs	Locally adapted MVs	Modern varieties	
				Self-pollinated / Open-pollinated	F 1 Hybrid
Community seed banks	compatible and in use	compatible but not in use	compatible but not in use	compatible and in use	incompatible
Farmer-saved seed and community seed exchange	compatible but not in use	usually compatible with small farmers' seed needs	usually compatible with small farmers' seed needs	usually compatible with small farmers' seed needs	incompatible
Local seed multiplication and distribution	compatible and in use	compatible and in use	compatible and in use	compatible and in use	incompatible
Government/ MNC seed companies	incompatible	usually compatible with small farmers' seed needs	usually compatible with small farmers' seed needs	compatible but not in use	compatible and in use

Combination of seed varieties and seed systems that are:

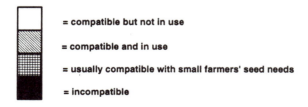

☐ = compatible but not in use

▨ = compatible and in use

▦ = usually compatible with small farmers' seed needs

■ = incompatible

Diagram 3.2: Seeds and seed suppliers: interactions and compatibilities

is discussed in Appendix 1.

Seed quality is a sixth technical parameter with a significant influence on farmers' and seed organisations' decisions. Unlike many goods, the genetic and physiological quality of seed is not intrinsically apparent, being revealed only at harvest, i.e. after it has already been used. Therefore systems of variety release and seed certification (see Appendix 1) have been established to deal with this problem. These impose delays and costs on seed suppliers, which have to be passed onto seed users. Furthermore, although they should provide safeguards for seed users, poor storage and handling after certification may reduce quality significantly and thus they may be of little tangible benefit in practice.

The precise influence of each of these technical parameters depends on the specific context of MV seed production and seed use. With regard to seed use, the cropping pattern and farming system will determine the portfolio of crops for which seed sourcing decisions are being made and the variety attributes being sought (high potential yield, low input requirements, storability, etc.). As regards MV seed production, the operational objectives of seed suppliers will determine the relative importance to them of maximising profits and minimising costs, and thus of the technical parameters outlined in Table 3.1.

However, some general interactions and compatibilities between different types of seed and types of organisation can be identified. These are outlined in Diagram 3.2. This shows the interactions between the functions that formal sector seed organisations aim to perform (and so their operational structures) and the technologies used within communities in CDR areas. It also shows the influence of these interactions on the ability to ensure a regular supply of appropriate varieties to CDR farmers.

Clearly, some types of seed and organisations are incompatible. These are represented by the shaded boxes in Diagram 3.2. For example, communities wishing to use seed of hybrid varieties are unlikely to be able to meet their seed needs through saving seed on-farm because of the difficulty of maintaining separate parent lines on small plots. By the same token, national seed companies are unlikely to have the capacity and motivation to collect and multiply farmers' varieties, preferring instead to concentrate on seed of a limited number of modern varieties. However, other combinations appear to be compatible, but have been neglected to date. These are represented by the blank boxes in Diagram 3.2. Such combinations thus include community seed systems working with farmers' varieties, and community seed banks working with enhanced farmers' varieties and locally adapted modern varieties. In general, formal sector seed organisations have set up parallel systems for local seed multiplication and distribution, rather than working with existing community seed systems.

One important point to note is the influence of government policy: an interaction may be possible from a technical and organisational point of view, but policy directives may expressly forbid it. For example some countries consider that the incremental yields possible from hybrid maize are so superior that they ban the sale of open-pollinated maizes, which effectively precludes any community level seed multiplication for maize.

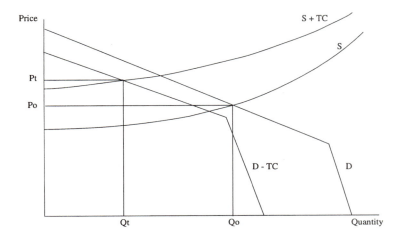

Diagram 3.3: The market for MV seed in Africa

3.3 The Market

Whilst commercial farmers' demand for MV seed is strong, MV seed is more problematic for farmers in CDR areas – who constitute potentially the largest market in many African countries. These problems are the result of four characteristics of MV seed as a commodity:

1. there are two readily available **substitutes** for MV seed: farm-saved seed and seed obtained through the community seed system. In practice, these are often simply grain saved from harvest rather a special seed crop, but they are substitutes in farmers' eyes;
2. this is partly because the value of a particular package of seed is not visible by looking at it: the **value is hidden** until the seed has germinated and the crop is growing in the field;
3. seed is not purchased for its own intrinsic value but as an intermediate input in the production process: MV seed must produce a demonstrable increase in the quality or quantity of the harvest *under farmers' conditions* for them to be willing to buy it;
4. seed organisations have to produce seed for numerous different crops and varieties in order to satisfy CDR farmers' demand, and seed being this **highly differentiated** a commodity increases production and distribution costs.

In Africa, transactions costs in the market for MV seed can be particularly high both for CDR farmers and for seed organisations. Farmers encounter the considerable costs of acquiring information about how particular seed performs. They also face the moral hazard of possibly being sold inappropriate or poor quality seed. Seed organisations, for their part, also meet with high costs of information in discovering CDR farmers' complex seed requirements. Their outlays are further augmented by the extra transport and storage costs incurred in satisfying CDR farmers' seed requirements, namely: having to provide multiple varieties of seed in small amounts at a very specific time of year because CDR farmers' demand for MV seed is significantly affected by seasonal variations; and, carrying stocks sufficient to meet uncertain and fluctuating demand. The diversity of reasons why farmers in CDR areas may wish to obtain seed from off-farm challenges formal suppliers, and thus increases their costs of research and seed production, as well as their transactions costs in learning about farmers' demands and dealing with uncertainty.

In addition to steep transactions costs, formal sector seed suppliers – whether they are public or private sector organisations – have found it difficult to supply CDR farmers with useful and appropriate modern varieties. As we saw in Chapter 2, most formal plant breeding has been directed at producing a limited portfolio of stable varieties selected to produce high yields in response to high inputs, suitable for farmers in areas of good soils, and good access to irrigation water and chemical fertiliser. In contrast, farmers in CDR areas require multiple varieties of the same crop, and varieties which perform well even under low-input conditions.

Further problems affect the supply of modern varieties of self-pollinated crops by the formal sector. There is the possibility of the farmer-purchaser multiplying the seed further on-farm and sharing the benefits with non-purchasing relatives or neighbours. At present, few seed organisations in Africa are able to enforce intellectual property protection.

Thus the market for MV seed in Africa exhibits some chronic symptoms of market failure. Diagram 3.3 illustrates the problem. Even if a modern variety appropriate to the farming system in question exists, the demand for MV seed is kinked: at prices below the cost of using own-saved seed (P_{os}), CDR farmers will use MV seed, and demand will be relatively inelastic since the area planted will be little affected by prices of MV seed. At prices above the opportunity cost of using own-saved seed, the demand for MV seed becomes elastic since few CDR farmers are willing to pay more than a small premium over the cost of saved seed for purchased seed.

For both the demand and supply schedules, the curves net of transactions costs (TC) have been drawn. Transactions costs depress the effective level of both the amount of MV seed supplied and the demand for it at any given price. The curves are not quite parallel: for suppliers the transactions costs diminish as the scale of operations increases, yielding economies of scale in information, storage, etc; for farmers in CDR areas, those who are better-resourced – for whom the benefit of using MVs is sufficient to justify paying higher prices – are generally better-informed about the attributes and sources of supply of the available MVs and suffer less moral hazard (for example, they have the power to pursue grievances).

The effects of the high transactions costs incurred both by buyers and vendors are clear to see: the outcome (quantity Q_t traded at price P_t) involves less MV seed being traded at a higher price than the socially optimal outcome in a market with no transactions costs (quantity Q_o traded at price P_o). Market imperfections thus cause clear losses of producer and consumer surplus and explain why, for farmers in CDR areas in Africa, it is rare to find formal sector seed organisations regularly supplying MV seed. (The exceptional case of hybrid maize is discussed in Appendix 1.)

Community seed systems have a number of advantages over the formal seed sector in CDR areas, because in these systems the above imperfections do not operate or are much reduced. There is no moral hazard involved in obtaining seed through community seed systems, because households usually know the person supplying seed to them and will have seen the crop from which the seed is supplied growing before harvest. Equally importantly, through community seed systems households are able to obtain seed of their preferred varieties, which they know to be adapted to their particular production conditions. And individuals and households supplying seed can charge lower prices because they do not face the additional transport, storage, seed certification and information-sourcing costs of the formal sector seed suppliers. But perhaps most importantly of all, a wide range of exchange mechanisms can be used to obtain seed, in addition to cash sales. These non-cash alternatives are an important means of giving a wide range of socio-economic groups access to seed.

It is therefore hardly surprising that, as we saw in Chapter 2, the community seed system continues to supply up to four times more seed than the formal seed sector in Africa.

Chapter 4

A Framework for Seed Sector Analysis

The preceding Chapters have shown us that there is now considerable pressure on the African seed sector to become more efficient, to become more participatory and to supply varieties that are more useful to farmers in CDR areas. We saw evidence from many different countries and contexts in Africa which points to various reasons why formal sector seed organisations can be unable or unwilling to meet CDR farmers' seed needs. This evidence leads us to question the two prevailing hypotheses on which much current seed sector development work is based in Africa, namely that:

1. the most important requirement is to increase the efficiency (reduce costs and/or increase revenue) of formal sector seed organisations;

2. the best way to increase efficiency is to transfer the ownership and control of formal sector seed organisations from the public sector to the private sector.

Instead, the evidence gives us reason to believe that structural and organisational change in the African seed sector needs to be much more fundamental if widespread and long-lasting improvements in performance are to be achieved. In this Chapter, we develop a framework for analysis which will allow us to test this assumption.

The framework presented in this Chapter is not intended to guide the choice of seed system to set up. Rather, it is intended to assess the performance of existing seed systems operating in a given country, region or project. It guides those conducting the analysis through deciding what functions the seed sector should perform; measuring how well it is currently performing these functions and establishing the reasons for poor performance.

4.1 Defining Seed Sector Functions

Clearly, governments, seed companies, voluntary organisations and farmers all have different definitions of desirable functions for the formal seed sector. Governments rarely state their objectives for the seed sector explicitly, for example, in national development policy statements, and this makes analysing the sector's performance potentially difficult. Nonetheless, it is fair to say that nowadays most governments' major concern in relation to the seed sector is to maximise at least possible cost the supply of good quality seed of appropriate varieties to farmers in CDR areas. This is with a view both to increasing individual farmers' incomes from agriculture, and to increasing national food security. In this context, therefore, two main functions can be identified for the formal sector:

1.   a **national development function**: the supply of the necessary quantities of good quality MV seed of the varieties preferred in CDR areas, in a timely manner to accessible locations at affordable prices and with appropriate extension support;
2.   an **economic efficiency function**: seed to be supplied by the formal sector in as efficient a way as possible.

4.2 Primary Indicators of Performance

Using these definitions of desirable seed sector functions, it becomes possible to identify measurable indicators of performance, as follows:

1.   the optimal **quantity of MV seed** needed annually;
2.   the **economic efficiency** of the formal sector seed organisation(s). Economic theory states that an organisation is operating efficiently if its level of output is such that average and marginal revenues and costs are equalised. However, this assumes that the organisation is operating in a perfectly competitive market, and that it is technically efficient in production. As these conditions do not hold in the real world, a substitute measure such as margin over costs may be more appropriate.

4.3 Explanatory Variables

In practice, the quantity of MV seed used and the economic efficiency of formal sector seed organisations are both often significantly below potential. Particularly in the case of public sector seed organisations, this is usually assumed to be the result of the organisations' internal inefficiencies and other supply-side distortions, and this results in the kind of initiatives to transfer ownership of seed companies to the private sector that became common during the 1980s. However, if we re-cap to Chapter 2, we find that there are six other variables, in addition to internal inefficiencies, which can also explain sub-optimal seed sector performance:

- *crop varieties*: the extent to which the available modern varieties are suitable for the farming system in CDR areas (in terms of both climatic conditions and farmers' preferences);
- *seed quantities*: taking into account actual sowing and replacement rates used by farmers compared with recommended rates; farmers' preferred seed bag sizes;
- *seed quality*: physiological (germination rates), as well as genetic quality of MV seed, at point of sale rather than ex-factory;
- *accessibility of seed*: ease of access to MV seed; timeliness of delivery;
- *agronomic advice*: availability of sales representatives, extension agents, or contact farmers to explain appropriate plant spacing, fertiliser application, etc. for MV seed;
- *seed prices*: the price of MV seed compared with own-saved seed, grain prices, and prices of complementary inputs such as fertiliser.

Thus, it may be that little MV seed is used by farmers in CDR areas because the varieties on offer are not those preferred by farmers, or because fertiliser is expensive and difficult to obtain, rather than because the formal sector seed organisations are inefficient in supplying MV seed.

4.4 Causal Factors

Again recalling the discussion of the nature of the seed sector in Chapters 2 and 3, we find that it is possible to group the factors causing poor performance in terms of these six variables into four categories:

Ecology and socio-economy

Agro-ecological factors May, for example, make it easy or difficult to save seed on-farm; or mean that the farming system in CDR areas is highly complex, so that many different crop varieties are needed; or mean that the production environment is unstable, so using MV seed is risky;

Socio-economic factors May, for example, mean that farmers in CDR areas want varieties with attributes other than high potential yield (for example, a particular taste or cooking quality), so MV seed is not attractive to them.

National policy

Macro-economic policy May mean that economic incentives favour one type of seed organisation over another (for example, co-operatives over companies); or mean that trade tariffs, exchange control, statutory wage rates, or low investment in transport and communications make it difficult to supply MV seed efficiently;

Agricultural policy May mean that factor costs (land, complementary inputs, etc.) are relatively high or grain prices are relatively low, both of which act as a disincentive to the use of MV seed;

Seed sector development policy May mean that, for example, controls on the retail price of MV seed, restrictive legislation concerning variety release and seed testing, and obligations to produce low margin seeds or to maintain strategic seed reserves impose additional costs on formal sector seed organisations.

Linkages between organisations

Linkages may be inadequate so that, for example, plant breeders are not aware of the variety attributes valued by farmers in CDR areas; distribution channels fail to supply farmers in CDR areas with MV seed and/or fertiliser at the right time and place; extension and credit institutions do not provide the necessary support.

Organisational efficiency

Finally, it may indeed be the case that the formal sector seed organisations themselves are not operating efficiently. This may be the result of, for example, lack of technical competence in seed activities; or poor internal management; or inappropriate allocation of investment and recurrent funding.

4.5 Methodology for Seed Sector Analysis

Having identified the components of an analytical framework for the seed sector, as above, the framework can be used to analyse performance in a four stage approach, as follows:

Stage 1 Primary indicators of performance: Find out what is the optimal supply of MV seed to CDR areas for national development purposes, and to what extent actual seed supply matches this. Find out what are target economic efficiency indicators for the formal sector seed organisation(s), and the extent to which these are currently being achieved.

Stage 2 Explanatory variables: Investigate the extent to which MV seed supply and organisational efficiency have been influenced by the performance of the formal seed sector with respect to: crop varieties, quantity and quality of available MV seed, timeliness and accessibility of MV seed supplies, availability of extension advice and the price of MV seed.

Stage 3 Causal factors: Establish the extent to which these variables have been influenced by external factors (ecology and socio-economy, national policy), compared with internal factors (organisational linkages in the seed sector, and the organisational efficiency of formal sector seed organisation(s)).

Stage 4 Performance analysis: Using the information obtained in Stages 1–3, identify the extent to which formal seed sector performance could be improved by facilitating internal changes within the sector, and the extent to which improvements in performance require external changes, i.e. to the context in which the formal seed sector functions.

A full national-level investigation, including data collection and analysis, could take up to four person months to complete. Ideally, such an exercise would be conducted in the context of a national effort at policy-oriented agricultural statistics gathering, processing and use, but where such a system is not in place or is already over-stretched, it could be carried out as an independent exercise.

Appendix 2 shows how this same method can be modified to carry out a cost-benefit analysis for individual seed projects or programmes.

4.6 Data Sources and Data Collection

The information needed for each stage in the analysis, and the best methods of obtaining it, are as follows:

Stage 1 Primary indicators of performance

1. *Quantity of MV seed needed annually*: area planted to each crop; recommended sowing and replacement rates per crop.

2. *Economic efficiency of formal sector seed organisation(s)*: in most cases, the only measure that formal sector seed organisations are prepared to release is their margin over production costs.

Cropped area is available from agricultural survey data; the agricultural extension service should have recommended sowing and replacement rates for MV seed. In most countries, the seed organisations' margins over production costs are widely known within government as they are used in setting retail seed price levels; otherwise, they can be computed from internal company reports. Box 4.1 shows the key components of this calculation.

Box 4.1: Tracing the build-up of costs through the seed sector

---

Seed multiplication

Basic/foundation seed procurement price

Crop husbandry costs	-	labour
	-	variable inputs (fertilisers, pesticides, etc.)
	-	supervisory management
	-	depreciation on machinery and equipment
	-	land rents
or	-	growers' premium
	-	supervisory management

Processing and storage

Transport from multiplication site to processing plant/store

Processing costs	-	labour
	-	variable inputs (fuel, packaging, treatment chemicals, etc.)
	-	depreciation on buildings and equipment
	-	cleaning losses, wastage, etc.
	-	processors' margin
Storage costs	-	labour
	-	variable inputs (fumigants, etc.)
	-	finance charges
	-	depreciation on buildings and equipment
	-	humidity and temperature control

Distribution and marketing

Transport from store to wholesale and retail distribution points

Marketing costs	-	variable costs (documentation, etc.)
	-	promotional activities
	-	maintenance of distribution points
	-	allowance for unsold seed, wastage
	-	distributors' commissions

~~~~~~~~~~~~~~

Critical seed prices in the cost build-up process

1.   Basic/foundation seed procurement price.
2.   Price of seed ex-seed farm/contract grower.
3.   Seed price ex-processing plant.
4.   Seed price to wholesale and retail distributors.
5.   Seed retail price.

Stage 2   Explanatory variables

1.   *Crop varieties*: modal cropping pattern in CDR areas; function of each crop economically and agronomically; varieties of each crop grown by farmers to fulfil these functions; how well the available modern varieties fulfil the desired functions.

2.   *Seed quantities*: adjusted calculation of quantity of MV seed needed, using farmers' actual sowing and replacement rates in CDR areas rather than recommended rates; farmers' preferences for large or small seed packages.

3.   *Seed quality*: physiological seed quality attributes desired by farmers in CDR areas; the extent to which formal sector seed suppliers provide these attributes; how the quality of MV seed at the point of sale compares with that of farm-saved seed.

4.   *Accessibility of seed:*
- *ease of access*: farmers' preferred type of seed outlet (public sector, commercial, within community, own-saved seed) and acceptable location/distance from household. How present formal sector seed outlets compare with preferences.
- *timeliness of delivery*: period during which farmers in CDR areas wish to be able to obtain MV seed, for each crop and season; whether MV seed arrives at this time in practice.

5.   *Agronomic advice*: how frequently farmers in CDR areas are contacted by seed company sales representatives, extension agents, or contact farmers; subjects discussed during these contacts; perceived utility of contact to farmers.

6.   *Seed prices*: MV seed prices at point of sale compared with: imputed cost of saving seed on-farm, prices of complementary inputs (fertiliser, pesticides, etc.), and farm-gate grain prices.

Most of the information needed in Stage 2 can only be obtained by conducting a farmer survey. The survey should be carried out in areas chosen to represent the major CDR agro-ecological zones and farming systems. Obviously the most appropriate survey technique depends on the particular situation and on the resources available. One possible approach is to start the survey in each area with a group interview at village level, to identify key general issues. This would be followed by household-level interviews with key informants to discuss these issues in more detail, using a format loosely structured to cover the six Stage 2 variables. In each household, both those responsible for resource allocation decisions and those directly involved in crop production should be interviewed. Households should be chosen to be representative of modal farms in CDR areas with respect to holding size, cropping pattern, labour availability, etc. as reported in recent agricultural surveys.

The evidence from the farmer survey needs to be compared with and amplified by existing secondary data sources, such as agricultural survey data, other published survey results and research work related to crop use and farmer seed preferences, etc. Interviews with staff at the key formal seed sector institutions will also be important. These will include:

1. *Ministry of Agriculture*: Department of Agricultural Research (relevant regional or commodity agricultural research stations, adaptive research teams), seed testing and certification agency, agricultural credit administration, fertiliser suppliers, planning units, selected field-level extension agents;
2. *Seed suppliers*: public and private sector seed companies, both multi-national and local; voluntary organisations;
3. *Seed distributors* (where different to seed suppliers): headquarters and depots of the national agricultural marketing parastatal, if one exists; wholesale and retail seed traders, both seed company agents and community-level traders.

The main aim in Stage 2 is to obtain as much quantitative evidence of formal seed sector performance as possible and to verify interpretations, where quantitative data is in short supply, by repeating the same questions to people working at different stages in the seed chain.

The timing of in-country data-gathering is important for work relating to the seed sector: the best results are likely to be achieved if survey work and institutional interviews can be conducted shortly before the main crop planting season, when seed needs will be paramount in the minds of farmers and seed organisation staff.

Stage 3 Causal factors

Ecology and socio-economy

- *agro-ecological factors*: climate, agro-ecology;
- *socio-economic factors*: size of farming population in CDR areas, both in absolute numbers and as a proportion of the total farming population; uses of crops grown.

National policy

- *macro-economic policy*: on economic structure (state involvement, free market, etc.), trade, exchange control, employment and wage rates, transport and communications, etc.;
- *agricultural policy*: on factor costs (including land tenure), input prices, producer prices, consumer food prices;
- *seed sector development policy*: on retail prices for MV seed, variety release and seed testing, formal sector seed organisations' roles in seed sector development (obligations to produce low margin seeds or to maintain strategic seed reserves, etc.).

Linkages between organisations

How well the organisations that make up the seed chain and package coordinate with each other.

Organisational efficiency

Costs and margins at each stage in the seed chain (as specified in Box 4.1); financial and other resources available to the formal sector seed organisations; degree of managerial independence; level of technical competence in seed activities; quality of internal management.

The information on external factors needed for Stage 3 is available from agricultural survey data and government policy statements. Information on organisational linkages has to be obtained by direct observation and staff interviews. Information relating to seed organisations' economic organisational efficiency can only be obtained from internal reports and staff interviews, with the permission of the seed organisation itself.

Stage 4 Performance analysis
No new information is needed for Stage 4.

Chapter 5

From Parastatal to Multi-National Subsidiary: What Role for the National Seed Company of Malawi?

5.1 Introduction

Malawi provides an example of what can happen when a parastatal seed company is sold to a multi-national corporation: the kind of divestment typical of many economic reform programmes in Africa. ADMARC, Malawi's national agricultural marketing parastatal, had the controlling interest in the National Seed Company of Malawi (NSCM) until 1988, when this was sold to Cargill. Cargill is the world's largest grain trading private company; it is also active in the seed sector in a number of countries in Africa and elsewhere.

Our main field work in Malawi, which we call 'the Malawi seed survey' for short, was carried out in 1990. As well as the institutional interviews and data collection, 25 small farmers were interviewed in three different agro-ecological zones: the mid-altitude maize/beans farming system and the high altitude beans/vegetables system, both in Central Malawi; and the semi-extensive upland maize system in Northern Malawi. The focus crops were maize, groundnuts and beans.

For all three country case studies, a second round of institutional interviews and data collection was then carried out in 1995.

5.2 Background[9]

Malawi has the twin disadvantages of being land-locked and without any significant natural resources other than fertile land. Agriculture dominates the economy, accounting for 35% of GDP, 80% of export earnings and the incomes of 85% of the population. The agro-ecology and sub-tropical climate are both

---

[9] This section is based on information in Cromwell (1992b) and various issues of *Africa Economic Digest*.

favourable for agriculture, and about 50% of Malawi's total land area of 90,400km^2 is cultivable. Agriculture is predominantly rainfed and the major small farm crops are maize, groundnuts, pulses and tobacco. However, with rural population densities already amongst the highest in Africa and population growth of 3.6% a year, agricultural cultivation has expanded significantly into fragile environments.

By the early 1980s, Malawi was still a very poor country, with a per capita GNP of just US$180, and external shocks and domestic policy problems meant the economy continued to decline. The war in neighbouring Mozambique was one of Malawi's most significant external problems: it meant that external transport costs increased dramatically and Malawi became host to large numbers of Mozambican refugees, equivalent to some 10% of Malawi's own population of 8.5 million by the late 1980s. On the domestic front, contrary to the popular image of the country, state involvement, through a few large, quasi-public institutions, was substantial in many areas of the economy until the mid-1980s.

Malawi has had a continuous history of economic reform since 1979 and was successful in moving towards greater macro-economic balance during the 1980s. By 1990, the general consensus was that Malawi's economy was returning to growth. The main objectives of agricultural policy reform during the 1980s were to increase producer prices, liberalise produce marketing (including restructuring ADMARC), and remove fertiliser subsidies. However, the real value of producer price increases was eroded by increased input costs, and private traders did not move into crop marketing as much as expected, due to lack of credit and infrastructure; the effect of those that did was generally to increase inter-seasonal variation in market prices. So by the end of the 1980s, the reforms had not yet had a measurable impact on the underlying structural problems in Malawi's agricultural sector: the basic problems remained of undiversified production, small farm sizes, lack of capital and lack of access to credit and improved technologies.

5.3 Small Farmers

About 20% of Malawi's cultivable land is used by large-scale commercial estates, primarily producing tobacco and tea (Government of Malawi, 1987). On the rest, there are a smaller number of commercialised small farmers with good access to credit, inputs and extension advice; and up to 1.2 million farmers on tiny farms (50% less than 1ha), many of whom do not produce enough food for their own domestic needs, and who have largely not been able to benefit from the government's National Rural Development Programme because of their lack of resources.

The small farm size dictates the production strategies that these farmers (hereafter called 'small farmers' for short) can pursue. First, the bulk of farmland is allocated to producing staple foods: 70% of the small farm area is down to maize. Groundnuts are important in many areas, covering up to 20% of cultivated land, and beans cover around 10% of the area. Up to 30% of total area is intercropped, primarily maize with groundnuts and pulses.[10] There is considerable inter-annual variation in the proportion of land planted to each crop, primarily in response to changing producer and input prices: Malawian farmers are highly price-responsive (Dean, 1966).

Given the dominant role of maize, the basic good agronomic practices for maize (early planting, appropriate plant populations, early weeding) are well-known and observed by the majority of small farmers. So management standards are considerably above average for the eastern and southern African region, except with respect to early weeding: although the benefits are known, small farmers find it difficult to carry this out in practice because the most widely grown groundnut variety has a long growing season, and so needs early planting and weeding, thus creating labour requirements which clash with those for maize.

The dominance of maize leads to a common set of constraints facing the majority of small farmers:

1. Availability of plant nutrients: small farmers are aware of the value of additional plant nutrients, however access is problematic for them; there is little intercropping of legumes; the livestock populations on the small farms are too low to provide sufficient organic manure; and about 70% of small farmers do not have sufficient cash resources to pay for chemical fertiliser. Consequently, in the late 1980s only 13% of small farmers with less than one hectare of land used any fertiliser at all (World Bank, 1989).

2. Shortage of labour: most cultivation is done by hand because there is little economic benefit to ox-ploughing on such small holdings. During the first few weeks of the growing season, the dominance of maize and groundnuts in the cropping pattern bunches the tasks of planting and weeding together, but most small farmers do not have sufficient resources to employ extra seasonal labour. Therefore, they concentrate on planting maize and this delays maize weeding and fertiliser applications and groundnut planting, and reduces yields as a result.

In this situation, between 75% and 95% of Malawian small farmers cannot meet their staple food needs from their own holdings. The majority do not sell any significant quantities of agricultural production either (or they sell at harvest to obtain cash for school fees and other essentials and have to take emergency measures later in the season to obtain food needs). They are therefore net sellers of their own labour, to provide supplementary food.

---

[10] These figures are taken from the 1987 Annual Survey of Agriculture conducted by the Ministry of Agriculture.

5.4 The Seed Sector

5.4.1 The formal sector

The first locally bred maize hybrid started distribution in 1959. In 1971, the government decided the seed sector should be organised on a commercial basis, so MV seed started to be sold at economic prices. By 1978, MV seed was being produced for maize, groundnuts, beans, sunflower, grasses, pasture legumes and tobacco. Given this progress, it was decided to establish a national seed company, which would operate on commercial lines as an autonomous subsidiary of ADMARC. The National Seed Company of Malawi started operating in 1980.

Responsibilities for the different stages in the seed chain were allocated as follows: plant breeding and production of new varieties remained with the Department of Agricultural Research; variety evaluation and release went to NSCM and the government Variety Release Committee; basic seed production went to NSCM, supervised by the Seed Technology Unit (now known as Seed Services); MV seed production went to NSCM using contract growers; quality control went to the STU; processing and storage went to NSCM; and distribution (except factory gate sales to large purchasers) went to ADMARC. Storage of the national seed reserve also went to NSCM.

The only major change to this division of responsibilities during the 1980s was the introduction of the Smallholder Seed Multiplication Scheme (SSMS) in the mid-1980s. The aim was to reduce seed production costs and encourage crop diversification by involving small farmers in the production of MV seed for self-pollinated crops. The SSMS is managed by the Agricultural Development Divisions (ADDs), the eight area-based agricultural development projects that cover Malawi.

5.4.2 The informal sector

As shown in Table 5.1, the informal sector was an important source of seed for crops other than hybrid maize for many small farmers in Malawi during the 1980s. As we shall see later in this Chapter, this was not because the informal sector was the preferred source of seed in all cases, but because small farmers faced difficulty in obtaining seed from the formal sector.

An important finding of the Malawi seed survey was that small farmers can be categorised into different groups on the basis of how seed secure they are. Table 5.2 shows the results by crop for the survey farmers. Only a tiny minority of growers recycled hybrid maize seed. Most farmers had secure seed supplies for local maize and groundnuts, obtaining seed off-farm only at times of crisis, if at all. For beans, many farmers used off-farm sources, but mainly simply to change variety. Growers of groundnuts and beans sourcing off-farm tended to use more than one source; maize growers, both local and hybrid, tended to use only one source.

Table 5.1: Sources of seed used by Malawi survey farmers (%)

	Local maize n=25	Groundnuts n=18	Beans n=21
ADMARC	24	(44)	(43)
Saved	68	78	90
Relatives	(20)	(11)	(29)
Neighbours	(24)	(33)	(43)
Local markets	(4)	-	(33)

Source: Malawi Seed Survey, 1990

Notes: (1)   Main figures show percentage of survey farmers growing each crop that use each source as their primary source of seed.
          (2)   Figures in brackets show percentage of survey farmers growing each crop that use each source as a secondary source of seed.

A very small proportion of survey farmers were chronically seed insecure for all crops. However, the survey found that female-headed farms were significantly less seed secure than other farmers: 20% of female-headed farms were seed insecure and only 40% were seed secure or obtained seed off-farm only by choice.

Hoarding seed, and distributing outside the immediate family only to selected people, appears to have been fairly widespread during the 1980s, creating concern amongst survey farmers over securing access to off-farm sources of seed. For all crops, the majority of survey farmers obtaining seed from off-farm sources did not share it with others, this being most marked for hybrid maize seed.

Table 5.2: Seed security status of survey farmers in Malawi

	Percentage of survey farmers growing crop			
Crop	*Secure*	*Crisis*	*Choice*	*Insecure*
Local maize	52	28	12	8
Groundnuts	28	28	22	17
Beans	19	42	29	10

Source: Malawi Seed Survey, 1990

5.5 Seed Sector Analysis

5.5.1 Primary indicators of performance

National requirement for MV seed

Table 5.3 shows the low level of MV seed sales for maize, groundnuts and beans in Malawi during the 1980s compared with potential. The Ministry of Agriculture (MOA) does not publish recommended seed replacement rates for the non-maize crops but breeders in the Department of Agricultural Research suggest replacement every two years for groundnuts and every five to six years for beans.

ADMARC sales of NSCM seed covered a tiny proportion of the area cropped by small farmers: apparently no more than 10% for hybrid maize and less than 2% for beans. SSMS seed production was very small and mainly reserved for further multiplication.

Formal seed sector efficiency

Table 3.2 in Appendix 3 shows the margins in the formal seed sector in Malawi, Zambia and Zimbabwe in 1990/91, from which some conclusions will be drawn in the next three Chapters concerning the economic efficiency of the seed organisations involved.

In Malawi, NSCM failed to cover its fixed and variable costs of producing maize, groundnut, bean and soyabean seed (although greater profitability was achieved on other crops) and it failed to achieve its overall target 15% rate of return on capital.

Most seed for small farmers is made available through ADMARC. Between 1982/83 and 1986/87, ADMARC's total seed distribution costs increased by 300% but the total quantity of seed sold increased by only 200% (World Bank, 1986). ADMARC was re-organised in 1987 but costs continued to increase per tonne of seed distributed and internal problems with seed transport, handling and storage continued.

The margins in the SSMS in 1990/91 are shown in Box 5.1. Prices paid to small farmer growers for SSMS seed provided a relatively high margin over grain production valued at official minimum prices, but for some crops, particularly groundnuts, this did not compete with the producer prices actually offered by private traders. 'Operating' costs, such as Seed Services' field inspection and ADMARC handling and storage costs (SSMS seed is not processed), were not provided for, and the ADDs' operation of the Scheme was severely hampered by this. Where SSMS seed was available for sale, prices were the same as for NSCM seed distributed through ADMARC. However, SSMS production was very low.

Box 5.1: Malawi SSMS production costs and returns 1990/91 (MK per hectare)

In 1990/91 MK1 = US$0.37

Borne by ADD		*Borne by farmer grower*		*Compared with grain production*
Groundnuts				
Item	*MK*	*Item*	*MK*	*MK*
Inputs	100.00	Inputs	112.00	112.00
Field visits	14.60	Extra labour	27.25	nil
Price paid for seed	700.00			
Storage, handling	77.00	Transport from/to market	22.40	22.40
less		*less*		
Credit repayment	112.00			
Price received for seed	700.00	Price received for seed	770.00	630.00
Net cost	149.60	Net return	608.35	496.00
(per kg)	0.21	(per kg)	0.87	0.71
Beans				
Item	*MK*	*Item*	*MK*	*MK*
Inputs	285.00	Inputs	319.20	68.40
Field visits	14.60	Extra labour	39.95	nil
Price paid for seed	770.00			
Storage, handling	77.00	Transport from/to market	36.40	13.20
less		*less*		
Credit repayment	34.20			
Price received for seed	770.00	Price received for seed	770.00	270.00
Net cost	342.60	Net return	374.45	188.00
(per kg)	0.49	(per kg)	0.53	0.42

Source: Own calculations. For assumptions used in calculations see Appendix 4.

Table 5.3: Potential for MV seed use in Malawi

Crop/Year	1984/85	1985/86	1986/87	1987/88
Maize				
Cropped area ('000ha)	1,145.00	1,193.00	1,182.00	1,215.10
Area suitable for MVs	1,030.50	1,073.70	1,063.80	1,093.59
MV seed need (tonnes)	25,762.50	26,842.50	26,595.00	27,339.75
MV seed sales (tonnes)	1,663.83	1,626.12	1,031.24	1,593.00
Current market (%)	6.46	6.06	3.88	5.83
Groundnuts				
Cropped area ('000ha)	136.00	177.00	211.00	172.10
Area suitable for MVs	102.00	132.75	158.25	129.08
MV seed need (tonnes)	1,836.00	2,389.50	2,848.50	2,323.35
MV seed sales (tonnes)	1,933.16	2,615.92	3,212.62	
Current market (%)	105.29	109.48	112.78	
Pulses				
Cropped area ('000ha)	80.00	117.00	152.00	149.00
Area suitable for MVs	40.00	58.50	76.00	74.50
MV seed need (tonnes)	640.00	936.00	1,216.00	1,192.00
MV seed sales (tonnes)			27.30	
Current market (%)			2.25	

Table 5.3 cont.: Potential for MV seed use in Malawi

Crop/Year	1988/89	1989/90	1990/91
Maize			
Cropped area ('000ha)	1,271.00	1,280.00	1,350.00
Area suitable for MVs	1,143.90	1,152.00	1,215.00
MV seed need (tonnes)	28,597.50	28,800.00	30,375.00
MV seed sales (tonnes)	1,925.00	3,826.00	5,272.00
Current market (%)	6.73	13.28	17.36
Groundnuts			
Cropped area ('000ha)	140.00	48.19	69.98
Area suitable for MVs	105.00	36.14	52.49
MV seed need (tonnes)	1,890.00	650.57	944.73
MV seed sales (tonnes)	2,692.52	820.00	2,422.00
Current market (%)	142.46	126.04	256.37
Pulses			
Cropped area ('000ha)	215.00	215.30	190.98
Area suitable for MVs	107.50	107.65	95.49
MV seed need (tonnes)	1,720.00	1,722.40	1,527.84
MV seed sales (tonnes)	22.44	49.00	174.00
Current market (%)	1.30	2.84	11.39

Notes:
(1) cropped area from Ministry of Agriculture annual crop estimates data.
(2) area suitable for modern varieties assumed as 90% for maize, 75% for groundnuts and 50% for pulses.
(3) seed need calculated using sowing rate of 25kg/ha for maize, 90kg/ha for groundnuts and 80kg/ha for pulses and replacement annually for maize and every 5 years for groundnuts and pulses.
(4) seed sales from 1984/85–1988/89 = ADMARC records (blanks = no record); 1989/90–1990/91 = from NSCM records.
(5) current market shows percentage of seed need met by current seed sales.

5.5.2 Explanatory variables

Crop varieties

There are no detailed studies of the economic functions of the major crops grown by small farmers, although some work was started by the Ministry of Agriculture's Adaptive Research Teams (ARTs) in the late 1980s. However, the general consensus of opinion is that hybrid maize is grown almost entirely as a cash crop; groundnuts and beans are grown primarily for sale, although small quantities may be traded domestically; and local maize is the main food staple, with sales being made only when there are surpluses or to meet immediate cash needs for school fees, clothes, etc. Thus, high potential yield is important for crops often sold, such as hybrid maize and groundnuts; but other attributes can be more important for crops that are primarily consumed domestically, such as local maize and beans. Overall, the range and blend of attributes required for each crop can be very complex, in order to fit specific niches in the farming system.

Although there was a considerable amount of formal sector breeding work in Malawi from the late 1950s onwards, work to find out small farmers' variety preferences started only in the late 1980s. The outstanding success here was the release in 1990 of two flinty maize hybrids, *MH17* and *MH18*, to meet farmers' preference for hybrids that can be stored on-farm. Groundnut breeding work, in particular, remained directed towards producing high potential yield oil nut varieties and attached low priority to small farmers' needs for confectionary nuts for on-farm consumption and local sale.

Furthermore, during the 1980s Malawi's Variety Release Committee continued to operate a policy of limiting the total number of varieties of individual crops released, in the belief that too much choice for small farmers would not be helpful.

Table 5.4 shows the varieties of seed available to small farmers in Malawi during the 1980s. The range of hybrid maize varieties NSCM produced was large but the absolute quantities of three way crosses were much greater than of single cross hybrids. This is because the former are cheaper for NSCM to produce than the latter. Thus, regardless of the potential benefits, in practice small farmers often did not have access to their preferred *MH12* (single cross) hybrid maize varieties and had to use *NSCM41* or *R201/215*, which are three way cross hybrids. NSCM produced some groundnut and bean seed, but most of this was varieties suitable for the estate sector, or small quantities of source seed for the SSMS.

Due to problems with getting NSCM to produce seed of the MV beans bred by the National Bean Programme (NBP), at first the SSMS produced only *Red Canadian Wonder*, an imported variety. This main-season variety was of only limited relevance for areas where off-season bean production is important. There was no distribution of MV bean seed originating from Malawi until 1987, when the NBP gave one ADD some *Nasaka* for SSMS production. This took off

Table 5.4: Seed varieties available to small farmers in Malawi

Crop	*Released*	*Produced/imported by NSCM*	*Produced by SSMS*	*Other varieties grown by survey farmers*
Maize				
Top cross	MH17, MH18	MH17, MH18		
Single cross	MH12, MH16			
Three-way cross		NSCM41, R201, R215	nil	Bingo (LH11) (double cross)
Synthetic/Open-pollinated	Tuxpeno 1	Kalahari Early Pearl	nil	Askari (SV17), SV37
Composite	UCA (CCC), CCA, (CCD)	UCA, CCC, CCA	nil	Bantam, Kagolo, Thikinya
Groundnut	Chalimbana, Maripintar, Malimba, RG1, Chitembana, Mawanga, MG1	*Chitembana, Mawanga*	Manipintar, Mawanga	Kalisere, Kasawaya, Mwitunde, Charles
Beans	Nasaka (253/1), Bwenzilawana (373), Kamtsilo (4991/1), Sapelekedwa (600/1), Kanzama (97/1), Namajengo (336)	*Red Canadian Wonder, Longbow, Bonus, Harvester*	*Nasaka, Sapelekedwa, Red Canadian Wonder*	RCW, Thyolo, White Haricot, Sugar Beans, Maliya, Phalombe, Khaki, Mkharatsonga, Nanyati, Nagogoda, Chimbamba, Nyauzembe, Kalongalonga, Chizgama, Nyalubwe, Chaholi, also 'red', 'green', 'yellow', 'white' and 'black'

Note: *italic script* = not for sale to small farmers
Source: VRC, 1986; Malawi seed survey; NSCM, 1990

rapidly and SSMS production of *Sapelekedwa* and *Nasaka* followed in four ADDs.

However, all bean and groundnut seed produced under the SSMS continued to be sold to ADMARC for resale as source seed for the next seasons' SSMS, due to the relatively small quantities being produced, so no MV seed of these crops was available for small farmers to buy.

Thus, seed for many of the crop varieties that small farmers wish to grow had to be saved on-farm or obtained from relatives, neighbours, or local markets in the informal sector.

Seed quantities

Some very rough estimates of farmers' actual replacement rates were made by the Malawi seed survey; these are given in Table 5.5. As might be expected, the differences in the proportions of farmers replacing each crop are in line with the different recommended replacement rates but the overall levels are much below recommended rates. They show that although a clear majority of farmers obtained planting material off-farm at some time, only for hybrid maize did more than a third of farmers do so every year.

Thus the amount of MV seed required in practice by small farmers in Malawi was significantly below the theoretical potential indicated in Table 5.3. Nonetheless, according to the seed survey results, demand still outstripped supply in the 1980s. Half the survey farmers considered hybrid maize seed was always in short supply. Only one third of farmers considered bean seed was always in short supply, but this assessment included availability from the informal sector. Groundnut seed availability seemed to be a problem for the greatest proportion of survey farmers: over two thirds considered groundnut seed was always in short supply. The apparent over-supply of MV groundnut seed compared with area planted shown in Table 5.3 suggests that a proportion of MV groundnut seed was, in practice, purchased for consumption as food.

Thus, in the 1980s the seed supply problem in Malawi was severe and one of the major constraints to greater seed uptake. NSCM's contract growers experienced problems in meeting both target yields and target hectarage for maize

Table 5.5: Malawi survey farmers' seed replacement habits (% of farmers)

Crop	Replace periodically+	Replace every year
Hybrid maize	100	92
Groundnuts	66	22
Beans	86	10

Note: + = within last 5 years
Source: Malawi Seed Survey, 1990

seed, so NSCM maize seed production continued to be lower than the estimated quantity requested by the ADDs. And NSCM did not produce any MV seed for the small farm sector for other crops.

However, the requests ADDs made were not always related to previous sales. Furthermore, allocations made by the Ministry of Agriculture to the ADDs did not always reflect the requests originally made by the ADDs – particularly for hybrid maize, which tended to be over-supplied, and composite maize seed, which tended to be under-supplied.

Thus, farmers ended up sourcing seed from the informal sector even when this was not their preferred source, as we shall see below.

Pack size is an ancillary issue relating to the quantity of seed supplied. Interestingly, the 10kg packs in which all MV maize seed is supplied in Malawi were considered by the survey farmers to be inconveniently small rather than too large. The minimum quantities in which MV seed of other crops is supplied did not attract the same comment; however, the 1kg minimum quantity in which individual varieties of beans can be bought from ADMARC attracted complaints as a number of farmers wished to buy small quantities of a number of different varieties.

Seed quality

The quality of hybrid maize seed reaching survey farmers seemed to be good, despite minor problems with weevilling and rotten kernels. In fact, the quality of all NSCM and SSMS seed was good, even though the latter officially receives only 'approved' status rather than being classed as certified seed. Farmers appeared to have good faith in the quality of seed provided at ADMARC selling points. The main problem with regard to seed quality during the 1980s appeared to be the over-stretching of Seed Services: its budget was insufficient to ensure the timely provision of the full range of field inspection services required.

Most groundnut and bean seed used on-farm is in fact grain. The Malawi seed survey found that the quality of this 'seed' was variable: bought-in groundnuts were often of higher visual quality than those saved on-farm; the opposite was true for beans.

Access to seed selling points

During the 1980s the only source of hybrid maize seed available to small farmers in Malawi was ADMARC selling points. For groundnuts, most survey farmers' stated preference was to get seed from ADMARC. However, in practice a proportion had to use seed saved on-farm rather than their preferred source. For beans, substantially more survey farmers actually used on-farm sources than cited this as their preferred source. Of the off-farm sources, local people and local markets were preferred and used by many farmers, but, importantly, most farmers who sourced seed off-farm because of some kind of domestic crisis used ADMARC instead of local sources. Thus, a greater proportion of survey farmers, very substantially so for beans, relied in practice primarily on seed saved on-farm than gave this as their preferred source. This supports the premise that in the 1980s there were major practical constraints limiting the use of off-farm seed sources for small farmers in Malawi.

Most survey farmers did not seem to consider distance to ADMARC depots an important influence on their decisions concerning seed sourcing. For preferred bean varieties, in particular, respondents travelled up to 30km to source seed, which is considerably in excess of average distances to ADMARC selling points: most survey farmers were within 5km of their nearest ADMARC selling point. Over half the farmers had to travel further following ADMARC's 1987 retrenchment, but the modal increase in distance was only 2km.

As explained above, little SSMS seed was available for purchase by small farmers during the 1980s, so accessibility questions did not arise.

Local sources, either individuals or markets, were the nearest source of groundnuts for planting for most survey farmers. ADMARC selling points were the next nearest and relatives the furthest. There were no significant differences in this between geographical areas. The distance travelled to obtain beans for planting from local sources and from relatives was significantly greater than for other crops.

In general, as individual farmers using ADMARC selling points tended to travel to the same limited number of selling points that were within reach locally to source seed for all crops, there was no variation in distance of selling points used for different crops. Relatives, used primarily for groundnuts and beans, were furthest away, perhaps because survey farmers were prepared to travel to get a particular type of seed or to take advantage of kinship obligations to obtain seed. Local sources for groundnuts were the nearest, and nearer than ADMARC selling points. They were quite far away for beans, perhaps because survey farmers were willing to travel further to source the range of varieties needed to maintain bean portfolios.

The survey farmers evaluated different potential sources of seed using a clear and consistent range of criteria which was ranked, similarly for all crops, as: reliable availability of seed; 'fair' prices (compared with the bench-mark of official seed retail prices); good seed quality; availability of preferred varieties; and timely delivery. Interestingly, distance to selling points did not rank as an important criterion influencing choice of seed source. In addition, there were certain special criteria for individual crops: option to purchase out of shell for groundnuts; option to purchase small quantities of individual varieties for beans; and availability of credit for hybrid maize seed purchases.

Against survey farmers' criteria, the performance of the formal sector compared with informal sector seed sources was assessed as being good on price and availability of credit, and good on freedom of access and seed quality. It was considered to perform poorly compared with informal sector sources on reliability of availability, timeliness of delivery and availability of preferred varieties. This assessment was common across all crops. Crop-specific disadvantages included the rationed access to hybrid maize seed at many ADMARC selling points (particularly where available seed was reserved for credit recipients), and the 1kg minimum purchase limit as it affected purchases of beans for planting. On the plus side, ADMARC's provision of groundnuts out of shell was considered to be an advantage.

This assessment translates into a clear set of preferences relating to seed source. Except for hybrid maize (because it has to be replaced every year for agronomic reasons and was available only from ADMARC during most of the 1980s), farm-saved seed was preferred for all crops, the reasons cited being that cash is not required and the variety is known. The formal sector was the next best source, in survey farmers' estimations, for groundnuts. But there was a clear preference for local sources for beans.

There seemed to be some connection between the nature of seed need and the seed source usually used. Purchases from ADMARC on credit were important for 'crisis' farmers growing groundnuts and beans and an important source generally for hybrid maize. ADMARC was not, however, an important source for groundnuts and beans growers sourcing off-farm by choice, nor for local maize growers.

These preferences can be compared with the actual sources used, as shown in Table 5.1.

Timeliness of seed delivery

A wide range of answers was given concerning what time of year survey farmers wished to have hybrid maize seed ready, from at harvest (June/July) to December: this did not appear to be related to their geographical location. The modal answer was September/October. A number of respondents mentioned specifically that they would like to be able to buy seed when selling their produce (i.e. in June and July) to ease their cash flow problems. Local maize was not included in this part of the survey as local maize seed is always sourced locally.

The desired time of availability of groundnuts for planting ranged from August/September through October to November/December, with no clear mode. A wide range of desired times of availability of beans for planting was also recorded, from August/September to December, the modal response being November/December.

The late delivery of MV seed during the 1980s was primarily due to ADMARC's problems with co-ordinating transport from its regional depots to its field selling points. For example, in 1990 up to 40% of maize seed and more of groundnut seed had not reached ADMARC's selling points by mid-November. This late delivery was a critically important disincentive to more widespread use of MV seed by small farmers in Malawi.

Seed produced under the SSMS is sold by producers to their nearest ADMARC market as soon as it has been harvested and is stored there until the seed selling season starts. Therefore, the question of timeliness of delivery does not arise. However, as during the 1980s SSMS seed was mainly used as source seed for the next season, little was available for small farmers to purchase.

Thus, during the 1980s poor accessibility of MV seed forced small farmers in Malawi to rely on saved seed supplemented by informal sector sources.

Survey farmers' awareness of selection and storage techniques that can be used to save seed on-farm was low. For maize, most survey farmers planted grain from the granary when the rains started. They did not see the value of trying to maintain purity as there are so many local maize varieties and sources of cross-pollination. 40% of the Malawi seed survey farmers who selected seed early treated the selected seed, adding the pesticide Actellic (*pirimiphosmethyl*) to the sack containing the seed before storage. However, 30% of the others also applied Actellic to food grain (the recommended practice) thus including seed maize.

For groundnuts, the majority of survey farmers stored seed in the granary in shell, followed by de-shelling and selection and, for those farmers not selecting for immediate planting, subsequent storage in a pot, bag or gourd in the granary or in the house. Storing groundnuts in shell was seen as sufficient protection from pests and diseases by all farmers and no seed treatment was applied.

No survey farmer selected beans at planting; this may be because beans tend to be planted after other crops and farmers have one seed selection session for all crops in time for the earlier maize planting, in mid–late November. As regards seed storage practices for beans, insect pests such as bruchids are a major problem in Malawi. Accordingly, two thirds of survey farmers attempted to control pests. Of these, one third added ashes, 15% added only Actellic, and 15% added a mixture including Actellic, ashes, sand, finger millet chaff and blue gum leaves. The National Bean Programme confirms that ashes are just as effective a treatment against storage pests for bean seed as Actellic.

Agronomic advice

During the 1980s there did not appear to have been any extension work on the value of using selected seed, nor on on-farm seed selection and storage techniques.

At this time the MOA *Guide to Agricultural Production*, the annually updated handbook for all agricultural staff in Malawi, contained little reference to seed care other than instructions to tell farmers to replace seed of composite and hybrid maizes regularly and to use certified seed of modern varieties of maize. Use of off-farm seed sources for other crops was proposed only for those farmers not self-sufficient in seed. Advice on on-farm seed selection was limited to local maize and groundnuts.

Similarly, Ministry of Agriculture field staff did not spend time promoting awareness of the differences between seed and food grain, or good seed selection practices on-farm. The benefit of using modern varieties was described in extension messages, and demonstration plots of modern varieties were mounted at some local extension offices and farmer training centres, but these must have had little relevance to the majority of small farmers who were in areas where there was no MV seed of crops other than maize available.

As described earlier, official extension advice relating to seed of non-maize crops was extremely limited. In practice, most survey farmers relied on local sources for information about seed care, particularly older relatives and respected local farmers.

Seed prices

Small farmers' real returns to using MV seed were lower than returns to using grain as planting material for non-maize crops during most of the 1980s, because of the minimal incremental yield obtained from using such seed under small farm production conditions. Towards the end of the 1980s the difference was reduced because seed prices and grain prices (the opportunity cost of seed saved on-farm and the real price of non-seed planting material purchased off-farm) converged (see Table 3.1 in Appendix 3).

In particular, MV maize seed prices increased substantially between 1989/90 and 1990/91. Because of this convergence, the influence of recommended seed replacement rates on relative returns to using seed compared with grain was minimal. However, in general, real returns to production for most crops declined during the 1980s as producer prices reduced in real terms.

For all crops, the majority of survey farmers cited lack of cash to pay for seed as a constraint to use of MV seed although, in practice, this did not deter nearly two thirds of the farmers from buying hybrid maize seed (this is probably influenced by the 30% price subsidy that operated during the 1980s).

Subsidies on the retail price of groundnut and bean seed were removed in 1987; maize seed continued to receive a 30% price subsidy throughout the 1980s. This was implemented by ADMARC selling seed cheaper than it bought it from NSCM; ADMARC was supposed to receive an annual subvention from the government for doing this but this did not happen in practice until after 1987.

The convergence of seed and consumer prices for groundnuts during the 1980s (see Appendix Table 3.1) explains why consuming groundnut seed as food was an economic course of action for farmers at this time. Malawi's experience seems to substantiate the common perception that it is difficult to organise economically viable MV seed production for groundnuts in economies with controlled prices.

5.5.3 Causal factors

Ecology and socio-economy

On the supply side, strong competition between tobacco and maize seed production, which require relatively high prices to be paid to NSCM's contract growers, and the prevalence of field and store bean pests in Malawi, which require formal sector seed production to be done more expensively in the dry season using irrigation, both add to the cost of producing MV seed in Malawi.

More fundamentally, on the demand side the basic problem with increasing the use of MV seed by small farmers in Malawi is the low incremental yield obtained from MV seed under current farm management conditions. Added to this, most of the available modern varieties provide a very limited range of the non-yield attributes required by small farmers. This can partly be solved by encouraging breeders to develop varieties that yield well under low input/low management conditions and varieties that provide other attributes. But as long as good agronomic management of non-maize crops is made difficult in Malawi by the competition of maize for scarce labour time and other resources, the incremental gain from this strategy is likely to be low.

Macro-economic policy

The de-control of prices and inflation of the 1980s combined to mean that NSCM's MV seed production costs increased faster than the retail prices the Company could charge for its seed.

The long-standing difficulty with contracting sufficient cheap transport from private hauliers, which resulted from the low level of transport infrastructure within Malawi and the foreign exchange difficulties associated with bringing in vehicles and spare parts, had a substantial influence on ADMARC's seed delivery performance during the 1980s.

The inability to find effective policy measures to encourage widespread participation in private trade outside urban areas meant seed distribution had to continue to be organised through ADMARC's market network. This imposed additional costs on providing seed nation-wide.

Many of ADMARC's problems during the 1980s stemmed from the influence of wider development policy objectives on the way the Corporation was originally set up. It was not originally expected to operate commercially and furthermore many additional development functions were added to its original mandate over the years, involving complex funding arrangements. Therefore until economic reform started, there was little reason for ADMARC to be concerned with its internal efficiency, and it was difficult for it to monitor this in any case.

Agricultural policy

Despite the partial removal of seed price subsidies in 1987, NSCM's retail seed prices declined in real terms over much of the 1980s, and this was an important factor limiting the Company's financial performance. It resulted from ADMARC implementing the MOA policy of keeping seed prices as low as possible and was related to the Corporation's own internal objectives: retail seed prices could have been kept low by continuing subsidies but, as ADMARC at that time had to bear the cost of seed price subsidies itself, it preferred to avoid them by limiting NSCM's price rises. ADMARC did this by using the controlling interest in NSCM that it had until 1988.

Thus price levels appear to have had a negative influence on the use of MV seed in Malawi during the 1980s. As we have just explained, this was not the result of high retail seed prices; rather it was the result of a combination of low official producer prices, high input prices, and the high cost of formal sector seed production and seed imports. For the SSMS, the strong price competition from private traders for groundnuts limited the attractiveness of the Scheme to small farmers.

The agricultural credit system that operated during the 1980s was another factor which seems to have adversely affected seed sector performance at this time. It seems that whilst only a minority of better-off small farmers used credit to finance seed purchases, it badly affected the smooth distribution of available stocks of seed from field selling points, through the requirement that no seed was sold until credit recipients had been supplied.

Agricultural policy more generally, via its influence on factor costs, producer prices and structural issues, was partly the cause of much lower than anticipated sales of seed during the 1980s, which adversely affected NSCM's financial performance.

Seed sector development policy

One problem with trying to direct formal seed sector activity in Malawi towards the needs of small farmers has been the lack of an explicit, coherent and influential seed sector development policy. When work first started in the early 1970s on organising a formal seed sector, various policies were formulated for dealing with the factors affecting seed sector performance. However, many of these were not followed through and important variables influencing the performance of the sector, such as agricultural prices, were allowed to be determined largely by non-seed concerns. There was no co-ordinated body with effective power to press for policies and actions favourable to the seed sector (the only such body, the Seed Technology Working Party, does not have executive authority). Furthermore, after the initial work in the 1970s, new initiatives to improve seed sector performance were fairly limited: the establishment of the SSMS was the main one.

For ADMARC, the major role in the seed sector assigned to it by government policy further added to the cost of the Corporation's seed activities. Its responsibilities included, for example, subventing NSCM's losses and carrying the major burden of risk associated with distribution of NSCM seed, whilst it was the majority shareholder in NSCM, and bearing the cost itself of providing NSCM seed nationwide at fixed, subsidised prices, of handling and storing SSMS seed and of supervising the distribution of seed on credit. Some of these arrangements were re-organised in ADMARC's favour in 1987 but it still had to meet the costs of SSMS seed and to co-ordinate with the ADDs on credit distribution, and there were problems with the practical implementation of its new subvention for subsidising, transporting, handling and storing NSCM seed.

Furthermore, the way the cost of the subsidy on maize seed was subvented to the Corporation did not provide incentives to improve internal performance: the subvention did not distinguish the seed price component from ADMARC's operational costs, and therefore the Corporation had no incentive to control the latter.

The creation of Malawi's Smallholder Seed Multiplication Scheme was an explicit policy response to the problem of producing MV seed of self-pollinated crops cheaply using NSCM. However, lack of follow-through in policy development since its establishment seemed very significantly to have hampered the Scheme's efficiency and the service it provided to small farmers. In particular, lack of funding meant that the quantities produced were very small. Therefore the SSMS had little impact on the overall availability of MV seed to small farmers in Malawi during the 1980s, and the Scheme was a drain on the general budgets of the ADDs operating it.

Linkages between organisations

The way NSCM's linkages with other organisations worked, especially with ADMARC and the ADDs, had an important influence on the Company's performance during the 1980s. In particular, the Company's fear of amassing large, expensive carry-over seed stocks due to reliance on the ADDs' over-optimistic seed estimates – which it did once in the mid-1980s with disastrous consequences – caused it to limit seed production. This contributed to the difficulty farmers faced in getting access to NSCM seed. Delayed payments for seed by ADMARC also increased NSCM's seasonal finance requirements during this period.

For the SSMS, the scope for improving the Scheme's linkages with other organisations, particularly the method of payment for Seed Services field inspection work, was not addressed.

Organisational efficiency

NSCM seems to have been able to operate along more-or-less commercial lines throughout the 1980s. Most of the time, it produced the quantities of seed that minimised its carry-over stocks; it produced more of the cheaper three way cross maize hybrids and less (none for the small farm sector) of the more expensive groundnut and bean seed; and it was able to share with ADMARC a very substantial proportion of its trading risk.

Although scope for marginal improvement in the Company's internal efficiency remained (in particular, greater involvement in marketing and distributing its own seed), it was factors external to NSCM – as described above – that had most influence on performance.

Decisions about the quantities of MV seed to be sold to small farmers, seed prices, and the geographical distribution of seed were all out of ADMARC's direct control during the 1980s: its main areas of responsibility were transport, handling and storage. In part, ADMARC's poor performance in these areas was a result of its lack of attention to its seed distribution activities. This lack of attention reflected the small size of its seed activities in quantity and value terms compared with fertiliser distribution and maize grain purchasing: for example, maize seed distribution costs were less than 1% of ADMARC's total maize trading expenses in the late 1980s (World Bank, 1986).

Thus, although ADMARC's mandate was to provide a seed service geared to the particular needs of small farmers, internal organisational problems added to the cost of its seed distribution activities and reduced the quality of the service it provided, particularly with respect to late delivery of seed to field selling points. The re-organisation of the Corporation in 1987 considerably improved its performance in general terms, but a number of problems remained. Those that most affected seed distribution were the lack of central co-ordination of secondary seed movement from regional depots and parent markets to field selling points; inadequate communication and transport arrangements at these selling points; and delays in responding to seed needs that arose during the selling season, caused by the bureaucratic organisation of ADMARC's management structure. Despite initial misgivings, the 1987 retrenchment had little impact in practice on the distances small farmers had to travel to obtain MV seed.

Although tentative estimates of the economic cost of SSMS seed suggest that the Scheme could be financially viable, a major constraint to the efficient operation of the Scheme during the 1980s was that it had no separate budget or staffing allocation at Ministry level or within the ADDs. The ADD staff responsible for operating the Scheme had a full complement of other responsibilities. The same applied to the Seed Services Unit, to whose existing workload were added SSMS inspections. Funding for Seed Services times and travel had to be taken from the ADD's general budgets; this limited it and made rapid disbursement difficult.

The other major problem with the operation of the SSMS during the 1980s was the scattered location of the growers' plots within each ADD. This added significantly to supervision and inspection costs and thus to the overall costs of the Scheme.

5.6 Conclusions

5.6.1 Seed sector performance during the 1980s

From the evidence collected during the Malawi seed survey, it seems that NSCM was operating relatively efficiently as a commercial company during the 1980s, even before Cargill's involvement. In fact, NSCM's strong performance in this area had in some respects a negative effect on the supply of MV seed to small farmers. NSCM minimised MV seed production for less profitable crops (non-maize crops) and varieties (single cross hybrid maize). It passed on the relatively high contract seed grower prices that it had to pay, in the form of high MV seed prices to ADMARC. And it minimised carry-over stocks from season to season, to the extent that on at least one occasion during the 1980s this compromised its ability to respond to an upsurge in demand for MV seed from small farmers.

The main impact of the change in formal seed sector organisation in Malawi in 1988, viz. Cargill's purchase of the controlling interest in NSCM, was to reinforce NSCM's commercial orientation. For the small farm market, after 1988 the Company focused exclusively on hybrid maize seed. Levels of investment also increased following Cargill's arrival, in a seed laboratory, in seed technologists to inspect the premises of NSCM's wholesalers and retailers, and in an adaptive research programme coordinated from Cargill's operations in Zimbabwe.

Other factors besides NSCM's organisational efficiency were important determinants of formal seed sector performance in Malawi during the 1980s. One significant influence appears to have been the inefficiency of formal sector organisations elsewhere in the seed chain: ADMARC, where the internal structure provided no incentive to improve efficiency; the SSMS, where its small scale of operations and continual under-funding made it more-or-less ineffectual; and the Ministry of Agriculture, where poor coordination between the central planning unit and the ADDs with respect to annual seed estimates resulted in alternate shortages and excessive carry-over of seed stocks.

Agricultural policy was also influential. The way the agricultural credit system was organised created avoidable blockages in the seed distribution exercise at ADMARC selling points. And the practice of maintaining relatively low real agricultural producer prices meant that it was rarely economic for small farmers to buy MV seed at the comparatively high real seed prices that pertained during the 1980s.

However, the single most influential factor appears to have been the limited benefits of using MV seed under the sub-optimal management for crops other than maize that prevailed in Malawi during the 1980s. This situation arose because of the inadequacy of family labour to meet the peak labour demand created by the dominance of maize at certain seasons.

5.6.2 Seed sector developments in the 1990s

Organisational change

The SSMS is still operating, and there are plans to expand it to include the production of open-pollinated maize seed, but it continues to have little impact on the availability of MV seed in Malawi. The main reasons for this are that the prices paid to SSMS seed growers do not attract sufficient small farmers into the Scheme, and ADMARC continues to be late in buying MV seed from those farmers that do participate in the Scheme.

Lever Brothers entered the formal seed sector in 1991, drawing on its links with its sister Unilever company in Britain, Plant Breeding International, and its existing network of detergent stockists. The company initially concentrated on distributing hybrid sunflower seed, to secure an alternative source of vegetable oil to groundnuts, but diversified into hybrid maize seed in 1992. However, it does not as yet have a large market share, because it has had problems contracting farmers to produce seed, it was not allowed to sell its seed through the ADMARC network until 1995, and it does not yet have an established reputation as does NSCM.

A number of voluntary organisations also entered the formal seed sector in Malawi, primarily in response to the 1992 drought. ACTIONAID, an international NGO working in Malawi, arranged with the government to buy up local maize in areas of surplus and distribute it as seed through the drought-relief network. In 1992 13,000 tonnes – 70% of it recycled hybrid – was bought, tested, packed and distributed to around one million small farmers. Although the government expressed some concern that maize grain was being distributed as seed, the exercise was deemed to have been valuable and was repeated in 1994, following a second poor harvest. The government subsequently issued a policy statement opening up the possibility of further NGO participation in the formal seed sector in Malawi in the future.

Ecology and socio-economy

The severe droughts that affected large parts of southern Africa in 1992 and 1994 were a major ecological factor that affected the seed sector in Malawi, by preventing many small farmers in the central and southern regions from saving their own seed. The formal seed sector was not able to distribute sufficient substitute supplies, and so, as we saw above, voluntary organisations filled the gap by supplying maize grain.

Further drought in 1995 meant that free seed and fertiliser were once again distributed. For example, in November 1995 British ODA announced that it would provide the equivalent of US$6.15 million to supply free seed and fertiliser to around 650,000 farmers in drought affected areas of Malawi.

Macro-economic policy

Following 30 years of single-party rule in Malawi, multi-party elections were held in 1994 and won by the United Democratic Front (UDF). As part of the election campaign, the incumbent party authorised large public sector pay increases, and the economy took some time to settle down following UDF's win. Thus real GDP declined by 9% in 1994, and various other economic reform programme targets were not met. This created a difficult operating environment for the formal seed sector.

Agricultural policy

Agricultural restructuring remains an important component of Malawi's economic reform programme and further liberalisation of agricultural marketing took place following the multi-party elections in 1994.

The government still announces producer prices for maize and other commodities, but these are now floor prices and private traders are able to buy and sell at any price above this. Despite the slow start to private sector participation in agricultural marketing in Malawi, ADMARC's core business of crop purchasing and fertiliser distribution is now facing increasing competition from private traders, as traders can sell fertiliser, and trade inside ADMARC selling points. Thus small farmers now have a direct choice between the national marketing parastatal and the private sector.

The fertiliser subsidy removal programme re-started in 1995, following its suspension in the late 1980s. This produced a dramatic 300% increase in nominal fertiliser prices between 1994 and 1995. Based on experience elsewhere in Africa – for example, in neighbouring Zambia – the negative effect of this on the amount of fertiliser used by small farmers, and therefore on the economic benefit of using hybrid maize seed, is likely to be substantial.

The disadvantages of operating Malawi's agricultural credit system through the Ministry of Agriculture (MOA extension workers had been responsible for assessing credit recipients and encouraging repayments) were becoming increasingly apparent in the early 1990s. Therefore, plans were drawn up to establish an independent credit institution using donor funding. However, during the 1994 election campaign, the main opposition party strongly criticised the existing credit system and, as a result, 90% of loans were not repaid that year. This created losses of some US$1.92 million, which the proposed new system would not have been able to service, so the entire agricultural credit system in Malawi collapsed in 1994.

Seed sector policy

The early 1990s was a period of major revision in the government's attitude towards formal seed sector development, from relying on public sector organisations and parastatals to encouraging private sector participation.

Policy reforms to permit the licensing of new seed companies were introduced and tax credits were provided for private investors in the formal seed sector. The variety release procedures were changed, to allow the release of privately-tested modern varieties. And work was started on establishing Plant Breeders Rights, both to encourage private sector plant breeding and to earn income from varieties developed by government breeders. The last remaining MV seed price subsidy (on maize seed) was removed, meaning that ADMARC was no longer a cheaper source of MV maize seed compared with other seed distributors.

Malawi ratified the international Biodiversity Convention in 1994. As far as the seed sector is concerned, this implies that the government should now be encouraging the use of a diverse range of plant genetic resources in crop production.

Linkages between organisations

As we saw earlier in this Chapter, linkages between the different organisations involved in the formal seed sector were relatively important in Malawi in the past. However, the increase in private sector activity in the seed sector in the 1990s has resulted in substantial vertical integration and thus a decline in the importance of these links. Most of the private seed companies have established their own breeding programmes, so modern varieties produced by government breeders are likely to become less widely distributed. Many of the seed companies also now have their own seed testing facilities, and have invested substantial amounts in seed marketing outside the ADMARC network.

5.6.3 Looking to the future

With the benefit of hindsight, we can say that in Malawi transferring the ownership of the seed company from the public sector to the private sector has not resulted in significant change in the performance of the seed sector. Changes in the way NSCM operated following Cargill's arrival were relatively minor changes of emphasis, not changes in overall direction.

However, other aspects of the relationship between governments, farmers and seeds in Malawi have changed dramatically. These changes have had a substantial impact on seed sector performance.

Liberalisation of national economic policies and of policies towards seed sector development have produced an increase in the number of organisations participating in the formal seed sector. This increased competition may reduce Malawi's comparatively high hybrid maize seed prices. Where widespread active private trader networks exist in other countries in Africa, for example in Kenya, seed distribution costs have sometimes been considerably reduced by handing over responsibility for some part of the distribution chain to the private sector (Gerhart, 1975). However, this has not been successful in all cases – as we will see with respect to Zimbabwe in Chapter 7. The increased investment in seed advertising and in the rural private sector seed marketing network may encourage the use of MV seed by reducing small farmers' information costs: as we saw above, in the past the MOA did not perform well in estimating demand for MV seed nor in providing relevant agronomic advice. Whatever the impact on MV seed prices, the liberalisation is likely to make it increasingly difficult for ADMARC to cover the cost of its MV seed distribution exercise, unless it is substantially re-organised.

Given that the effect of the agricultural credit system was to delay the distribution of MV seed to the majority of small farmers who were not credit recipients, its collapse may perversely have had a positive effect on access to MV seed for most small farmers. Nonetheless, the Malawi seed survey showed that credit was important for that minority group of farmers who fell into the 'insecure' category with respect to seed supplies, although they had not been able to make use of the previous system because of their lack of collateral. Perhaps in the future the Mudzi Fund, Malawi's version of the Grameen Bank that has been so successful with resource-poor small farmers in Bangladesh, could diversify to include loans for MV seed.

Three important seed sector performance issues remained untackled in Malawi in the mid-1990s. First, the organisational problems that were preventing the SSMS from realising its full potential, in terms of providing small farmers with cheap, accessible MV seed, had not been dealt with. Second, the implications for the formal seed sector of the recurrent droughts (most obviously, in terms of the new varieties and crops for which seed might be needed) had not been addressed. And third, Malawi still remained with the long-standing problem of how to make the use of MV seed for non-maize crops economic under prevailing small farm management practices.

Chapter 6

Seed Supply in Zambia: Life After the Provincial Co-operative Unions?

6.1 Introduction

Zambia has a national seed parastatal, ZAMSEED, set up at the beginning of the 1980s to operate at arm's length from government as a commercial company. ZAMSEED has not been the subject of reform itself, but its operations have been significantly affected by the liberalisation of agricultural marketing in Zambia that started in 1990 and was completed in 1993. ZAMSEED therefore shows the effect of this kind of phased agricultural market liberalisation, which has been a common outcome of economic reform in Africa.

The main Zambia seed survey was carried out in 1990. The focus crops were maize, beans, and groundnuts. For the farmer survey, which was carried out by the Adaptive Research Planning Team of the Zambian Ministry of Agriculture, 280 households were interviewed, selected from all three of Zambia's agricultural zones. 60% of the selected households were in the small farm areas.

6.2 Background[11]

Zambia is eight times the size of Malawi but, at 7 million in 1988, had slightly less than the same population at this time. The country chose to base economic growth around its mineral resources, and copper sales formed up to 90% of export earnings in the 1960s and 1970s. Although rural development was championed at the doctrinal level, small farmer agriculture was neglected in practice. At the same time, the economy became more and more heavily dependent on imports over time.

---

[11] This section is based on information in Gulhati, 1991; Young and Loxley, 1990; Mwanaumo, 1989; Ristanovic, 1989; Kydd, 1988; Norrby, 1986; and various *Africa Economic Digest* reports.

Zambia's main problem, since the mid-1970s, has been the terminal decline in foreign exchange earnings from minerals, caused by declining international prices, falling production and increased production costs. Government policy compounded these problems, through the failure to control exchange rates, wage levels and government expenditure, the failure to diversify, and great reliance on heavily-protected parastatals.

Between 1982 and 1985, Zambia's structural adjustment programme was supported by the IMF and other international donors, but Zambia's relations with the IMF were suspended completely between 1987 and 1990, due to policy disagreements between the government and the Fund. During this period, Zambia returned to a more controlled economy, following its own New Economic Recovery Programme. With the transition to multi-party democracy in 1991, the winning Movement for Multi-party Democracy (MMD) pledged to implement wide-ranging economic reform. The MMD has already introduced cash budgeting and started to reform the parastatal sector. In agriculture, consumer maize subsidies were withdrawn soon after the 1991 elections, and produce and input marketing liberalisation was completed in 1993.

Although 40% of Zambia's population relies on agriculture for its livelihood, agriculture's contribution to GDP remained unchanged at around 15% during the 1970s and 1980s. Agricultural price policy failed to encourage sufficient marketed production to supply the large demand for purchased food created by Zambia's large urban population and subsidised food prices; and for service provision the government relied heavily on the inefficient state marketing board, NAMBOARD, and the government-controlled Provincial Co-operative Unions (PCUs).

Nonetheless, Zambia's moderate sub-tropical climate and substantial surface water resources provide significant agricultural potential. Although nearly 80% of the total land area of 750,000km^2 is estimated to be cultivable, only 20% is cultivated at present.

6.3 Small Farmers

Zambia's 460,000 small farmers form 65% of the total farming population (GRZ, 1994). The small farm sector has a very wide food base focused around maize, pumpkins, groundnuts, beans, sweet potatoes and cowpeas, and small farm production accounts for a large proportion of the total marketed for all crops except maize, wheat and soyabeans, which are also produced by the large-scale commercial sector.

In Eastern Zambia, maize is grown by small farmers on the plateau land and sorghum and millet in the valleys, all three crops being intercropped with cowpeas and pumpkins. In the North, shifting cultivation is still common: trees are cut and burnt and the ash used to fertilise plots planted on a four-year rotation, with millet and cassava as lead crops.

The ending of guaranteed produce markets, coupled with the severe Southern African drought in 1992, led to a significant diversification by small farmers away from maize production to other crops such as sorghum and millet.

Although many small farmers use MV seed and fertiliser, at 10kg per hectare average fertiliser applications are very low and most farmers still work the land using hand hoes or animal-drawn implements. Problems dealing with the acidic and sandy soils in Northern and Western Zambia are common; these necessitate low-intensity cultivation. Working around the insecure input and crop marketing system has been a further problem for small farmers. Initially this insecurity resulted from parastatal inefficiencies; most recently, it has been the result of market liberalisation and the consequent withdrawal of services from many areas.

6.4 The Seed Sector

6.4.1 The formal sector

By the beginning of the 1980s, Zambia had many of the main elements of a formal seed sector in place and functioning: agricultural research, breeding and variety release procedures; a Seed Act regulating seed control and certification; a core of experienced seed growers, organised in the Zambia Seed Producers Association; and ZAMSEED to organise production, processing and primary distribution.

ZAMSEED was set up in 1981 to produce all Zambia's agricultural and horticultural seed needs, as part of a national policy change towards greater emphasis on domestic agricultural needs. It superseded the separate activities of the Zambia Seed Producers' Association (ZSPA) and NAMBOARD, which had respectively taken care of seed production and seed distribution since Independence. ZAMSEED is a commercial company but the government investment organisation, ZIMCO, and the Zambia Cooperative Federation together control the majority of ZAMSEED's equity and so have a strong influence on policy. Other shareholders are ZSPA; Swedefund, the Swedish funding agency; and the Swedish seed company Svalov, who are the managing agents. Bilateral aid from Sweden was significant in the seed sector in Zambia during the 1980s. This contrasts with the situation in Malawi, where British ODA's direct support for the seed sector ended in the late 1970s and the UK's Commonwealth Development Corporation sold their equity investment in NSCM to Cargill in 1988. It also contrasts with the situation in Zimbabwe, where there has not been any donor support for the seed sector.

ZAMSEED has a 1,200 ha seed farm for pre-basic and basic seed production but during the 1980s all certified seed was produced by contract growers. Most was produced by 150 ZSPA members, who are all large-scale commercial farmers located in Zambia's main maize growing areas. The Agricultural Sector Support Programme (1980–90), operated by government with Swedish support,

Table 6.1: Seed sources reported by survey farmers in Zambia (%)

	Maize *n=327*	*Groundnuts* *n=187*	*Beans* *n=210*
ZAMSEED	43	7	9
Saved	39	53	57
Exchange/gift	12	4	8
Buy locally	6	34	26

Source: Zambia Seed Survey, 1990

encouraged small farmer seed production, organised through the Department of Agriculture, and ZAMSEED started to use small farmer growers for some self-pollinated crops from 1986. During the 1980s the Seed Control and Certification Institute (SCCI) was responsible for quality control and certification. At this time ZAMSEED did not have a statutory monopoly but during the 1980s there was no other large-scale seed activity in Zambia.

Seed prices were controlled by the government. Until 1990, ZAMSEED saw itself primarily as a seed wholesaler and at the retail level MV seed was distributed through the Provincial Co-operative Unions and registered stockists. The PCU network was set up in the early 1980s under the central, government-controlled Zambia Cooperatives Federation (ZCF) and in practice operated more like a parastatal than a membership organisation. However, following the moves towards liberalisation of input and crop marketing which started in 1990, most of the PCUs stopped functioning, and ZAMSEED had to make fundamental changes to its seed distribution system.

6.4.2 The informal sector

Table 6.1 shows the main seed sources used by the Zambia seed survey farmers. This shows that at the time of the survey 85% of the small farm cropped area was still planted with farm-saved seed.

6.5 Seed Sector Analysis

6.5.1 Primary indicators of performance

National requirement for MV seed

Table 6.2 shows the potential for MV seed use for two of the major small farmer crops in Zambia during the 1980s. The data show that, after some years of relying on imports to make up the amount of seed required, by the late 1980s Zambia was seed self-sufficient for maize. However, the situation for groundnut seed was less satisfactory, and has deteriorated further in recent years; and for beans no MV seed was produced at all during the 1980s.

Formal seed sector efficiency

The production cost profile for ZAMSEED maize seed is given in Table 3.2 in Appendix 3. ZAMSEED's margin on seed produced was a modest 6% in 1990.

Table 6.3 shows ZAMSEED's net profits during the 1980s. Profits increased over the 1980s, to US$1.26 million gross in 1987, equivalent to 18% of revenue.

6.5.2 Explanatory variables

Crop varieties

Until the mid-1980s, there was only one maize variety suitable for small farmers, the single cross hybrid *SR52*. However, in 1986, Zambia's Department of Agricultural Research released eight maize varieties designed to provide stable, well-adapted, high-yielding varieties for early, medium and late maturity in each of the country's three main agricultural zones. They included single, double and three-way cross hybrids and two open-pollinated varieties.

During the 1980s ZAMSEED produced seed for most small farmer crops except cotton and tobacco. However, maize seed was the company's main product and much of the other seed was made available only on an *ad hoc* basis through individual development projects, which usually had to collect seed from ZAMSEED's headquarters in Lusaka. Furthermore, open-pollinated maize varieties accounted for less than 10% of maize seed sales, and the three way crosses *MM603* and *MM604* accounted for 60% of sales.

During the 1980s a majority of survey farmers used hybrid seed for maize production. In the Zambia seed survey, vegetables, groundnuts and beans were the other main crops for which MV seed was considered necessary by small farmers. However, the main reason given for needing ZAMSEED seed was shortage of seed on-farm, rather than the superior attributes of the available modern varieties.

Table 6.2: Potential for MV seed use in Zambia

Crop/Year	1982/83	1983/84	1984/85	1985/86	1986/87
Maize					
Cropped area ('000ha)	454.50	546.70	581.00	588.49	593.00
Area suitable for MVs	409.05	492.03	522.90	529.64	533.70
MV seed need (tonnes)	10,226.25	12,300.75	13,072.50	13,241.03	13,342.50
MV seed sales (tonnes)	8,350.00	6,200.00	6,890.00	7,305.00	8,870.00
Current market (%)	81.65	50.40	52.71	55.17	66.48
Groundnuts					
Cropped area ('000ha)	22.44	31.39	33.00	34.36	37.00
Area suitable for MVs	20.20	28.25	29.70	30.92	33.30
MV seed need (tonnes)	363.53	508.52	534.60	556.63	599.40
MV seed sales (tonnes)	44.00	10.00	12.00	12.00	9.00
Current market (%)	12.10	1.97	2.24	2.16	1.50

Table 6.2 cont.: Potential for MV seed use in Zambia

Crop/Year	1987/88	1988/89	1989/90	1990/91
Maize				
Cropped area ('000ha)	596.00	596.00	534.29	463.12
Area suitable for MVs	536.40	536.40	480.86	416.81
MV seed need (tonnes)	13,410.00	13,410.00	12,021.53	10,420.20
MV seed sales (tonnes)	10,405.00	13,500.00	13,342.80	7,181.65
Current market (%)	77.59	100.67	110.99	68.92
Groundnuts				
Cropped area ('000ha)	42.00	46.00	80.44	127.29
Area suitable for MVs	37.80	41.40	60.33	95.47
MV seed need (tonnes)	680.40	745.20	1,085.94	1,718.42
MV seed sales (tonnes)	10.00	12.00	7.80	8.12
Current market (%)	1.47	1.61	0.72	0.47

Notes: (1)   cropped area from DanAgro, 1987; Norrby, 1986.
         (2)   area suitable for modern varieties assumed as 90% for maize, 75% for groundnuts.
         (3)   seed need calculated using sowing rate of 25kg/ha for maize and 90kg/ha for groundnuts and replacement yearly for
               maize and every 5 years for groundnuts.
         (4)   seed sales from Erikson *et al.*, 1989. This includes imports of 1,500 tonnes, 1,500 tonnes and 4,000 tonnes of maize
               seed in 1983, 1984 and 1986 respectively.
         (5)   current market shows percentage of seed need met by current seed sales.

Table 6.3: ZAMSEED income statements 1980/81–1984/85 (ZK million)

Item	1981/82	1982/83	1983/84	1984/85
Revenue: Export	0.0	0.0	0.0	0.2
Domestic	11.2	13.0	12.3	16.7
Total revenue	11.2	13.0	12.3	16.9
Costs				
Local production	6.8	8.0	7.6	9.1
Imported goods	0.8	1.6	1.6	3.8
GROSS PROFIT	3.6	3.4	3.1	4.0
GROSS PROFIT (% of revenue)	32.1	26.2	25.2	23.7
Other costs				
Labour	0.3	0.7	0.9	0.9
Transport	0.3	0.6	0.6	0.6
Building maintenance	0.0	0.1	0.25	0.2
Sundry operating expenses	0.1	0.3	0.3	0.3
Research & development	0.0	0.0	0.1	0.3
Marketing & administration	0.1	0.2	0.6	0.5
Interest	0.2	0.3	0.1	0.4
Depreciation	0.1	0.1	0.1	0.2
Total costs	8.7	11.9	12.1	16.3
PROFIT BEFORE TAX	2.5	1.1	0.2	0.6
PROFIT BEFORE TAX (% of revenue)	22.3	8.5	1.6	3.6
Tax	0.6	0.3	0.0	0.0
NET PROFIT	1.9	0.8	0.2	0.6
ZK1 = US$	1.15	1.08	0.79	0.55

Seed quantities

There was a significant increase in the proportion of the small farmer area planted with MV maize seed during the 1980s, from 30% in 1981 to over 70% in 1988. The main reason for this was the release of a range of MVs that were appropriate to small farmers' needs. By the late 1980s ZAMSEED met all the effective national demand for MV maize seed; however, its production of non-maize MV seed remained very low.

Table 6.3 cont.: ZAMSEED income statements 1985/86–1988/90 (ZK million)

Item	1985/86	1986/87	1987/88	1988/89
Revenue: Export				
Domestic				
Total revenue	24.7	39.6	65.7	115.0
Costs				
Local production				
Imported goods				
GROSS PROFIT	7.2	15.7	12.6	35.3
GROSS PROFIT (% of				
revenue)	29.1	39.6	19.2	30.7
Other costs				
Labour				
Transport				
Building maintenance				
Sundry operating expenses				
Research & development				
Marketing & administration				
Interest	0.9	0.6		
Depreciation	0.4	0.2		
Total costs	20.0	31.8	54.0	108.2
PROFIT BEFORE TAX	4.7	7.8	11.7	6.8
PROFIT BEFORE TAX (% of				
revenue)	19.0	19.7	17.8	5.9
Tax	0.6	1.0	1.8	1.0
NET PROFIT	4.1	6.8	9.9	5.8
ZK1 = US$	0.32	0.13	0.11	0.12

Source: Erikson *et al.*, 1989

Nearly 60% of all MV maize seed sold in Zambia is distributed in small 10kg packs. The seed survey found there was a clear polarisation in farmers' attitudes towards pack size: 70% were happy with the 10kg packs, but 20% stated they wanted to use larger 50kg packs. Overall, however, few of the farmers interviewed visualised different pack sizes clearly and packaging was not specified as a major seed problem.

Seed quality

During the 1980s the seed quality provisions of Zambia's 1967 Seed Law were generally implemented well. SCCI provided an effective quality control service at a charge equivalent to less than 2% of total costs per kg of seed produced by ZAMSEED. Survey farmers ranked seed quality second from last in their list of seed problems.

Access to seed selling points

The PCU depots were the major access points for MV seed for small farmers during the 1980s. 80% of all farmers were within 10km of the nearest PCU depot (deemed to be within acceptable walking distance), so MV seed should have been easily available locally when the PCUs were functioning, but maize seed was the only MV seed line that they sold: most non-maize seed sales were made via a few local development projects, which severely limited the availability of non-maize MV seed. In addition, 65% of maize seed went to only three Provinces (Southern, Central and Eastern) and many varieties were available only in the higher potential zones. Thus physical access to ZAMSEED seed was severely limited for many small farmers.

Many survey farmers were familiar with the names of the newly released maize varieties but had no information about their local availability. Non-availability of ZAMSEED seed at depot level was ranked as the single most important seed problem by farmers in the seed survey, and the single greatest constraint to the uptake of non-maize MV seed.

Timeliness of seed delivery

During the 1980s, ZAMSEED and the PCUs rarely managed to move all seed out to the depots and stockists by October, farmers' desired planting time.

After the partial market liberalisation in 1990, late delivery was exacerbated by the PCUs' inability to obtain bank credit to purchase MV seed from ZAMSEED. Previously, the banks had been willing to provide bridging finance for the PCUs' MV seed purchases for the few months until the PCUs had completed their sale of the previous harvest and thus had income to clear the bridging loan. But after the start of liberalisation in 1990, the PCUs were no longer the sole authorised purchasers of small farmers' crops, so the banks became concerned that the PCUs might not generate enough income from crop sales to clear their bridging loan, and stopped providing this finance. The PCUs therefore had no money with which to buy MV seed in time for the start of the planting season. For example, by November 1990, the PCUs had bought virtually no seed from ZAMSEED and the company was US$10.9 million short on its normal trading position, US$6.2 million of which was needed to pay contract seed growers for 1989/90 production.

Agronomic advice

Less than half the survey farmers could identify the certification label on a bag of ZAMSEED seed and explain what it meant. Half said they did not know what ZAMSEED was, nor what it produced. When asked where they got their information on seed for the crops they were growing, 56% of survey farmers quoted tradition, family, neighbours and friends. Only 6% mentioned extension workers, although the use of extension advice varied between crops and was higher for maize and cash crops than for others.

Only 12% of the extension workers and PCU sales staff interviewed in the Zambia seed survey had received specialised seed training. 20% had no information on seed at all and, for those that had, it was mainly ZAMSEED variety description pamphlets. Only 18% could recognise all the information on the seed certification label on ZAMSEED bags, although most could list numerous crops for which ZAMSEED supplied MV seed. Despite this, most believed farmers were getting sufficient and appropriate information on seed issues.

Seed prices

The expense of MV seed was ranked as the second most important seed problem for survey farmers after poor availability of seed. Although the government controlled seed prices during the 1980s and took farm input costs into account when setting them, the need to provide contract seed growers with an acceptable margin and to limit the impact on consumer food prices meant that during the 1980s retail seed prices often provided farmers with little net economic benefit from using MV seed (see Appendix Table 3.2).

As in Malawi, it was not the price of seed alone but its comparison with other inputs costs and expected yield which was considered to have the greatest influence on small farmers. This was clearly illustrated in the 1970s when the maize variety *ZH1* was released with the intention of providing farmers with a cheaper alternative to *SR52*. This failed to be taken up, primarily because farmers were willing to pay the additional cost of *SR52* as this was judged to be sufficiently out-weighed by its additional yield.

More recently, the liberalisation of input and crop marketing produced further disincentives to the use of MV seed, particularly for maize, as the ending of guaranteed markets and subsidised inputs caused a diversification to other crops. ZAMSEED therefore needed to be able to respond with sufficient supplies of non-maize seed, which up to that time it had not emphasised.

6.5.3 Causal factors

Ecology and socio-economy

The wide range of agricultural zones in Zambia increases the number of varieties of each crop that need to be produced. This increases seed production costs for ZAMSEED and increases the need for marketing and extension advice about the relative merits of each variety. At the same time, this also means that the individual quantities required of each variety are small, so the economies of scale in seed processing and packaging are limited.

The large size of the country means that distribution is expensive, as seed has to be transported long distances. Costs are further increased by the poor level of development of transport infrastructure, which is limited by the high budgetary cost of building and maintaining roads to serve all Zambia's Provinces and Districts.

The socio-economic conditions of the majority of small farmers affect the demand for seed and the cost of supplying it. Demand is limited because the low level of management on many small farms, coupled with lack of extension advice and poor access to complementary inputs such as fertiliser, means yields are often significantly below potential (less than 1 tonne per ha for hybrid maize, for example, compared with 5–6 tonnes per ha on commercial farms) so there is little economic incentive to purchase MV seed. In addition, small farmers' complex farming systems mean that those farmers that do purchase MV seed require small quantities of many different varieties.

On the supply side, the political and economic power of the large-scale commercial farmers prevents ZAMSEED from charging higher prices to this group to cross-subsidise seed for the small farm sector. And in the past Zambia's large urban demand for cheap food limited the extent to which the government felt able to increase agricultural producer prices to provide an incentive for small farmers to use MV seed.

Macro-economic policy

Macro-economic policies which kept the Zambian currency overvalued for most of the 1980s made the imported inputs on which the seed sector relies more expensive than necessary. Further difficulties were imposed by the bureaucratic foreign exchange allocation system and, domestically, by the extremely high annual inflation rates. Minimal government investment in agriculture and in maintaining national transport and marketing infrastructure imposed additional costs, whilst the centralised, state controlled nature of retail trade in Zambia until the early 1990s made it difficult to rely on small-scale retail traders in rural areas as an alternative to the PCUs once liberalisation started to take place.

Agricultural policy

Throughout the 1970s and early 1980s, the government's reliance for national agricultural marketing services on parastatals and co-operatives of limited internal efficiency, its policy of restricting consumer food prices and its general neglect of small farm agriculture imposed substantial economic costs on small farmers and served as strong disincentives to purchasing MV seed. In addition, the real value of agricultural producer prices were badly eroded by inflation.

The policy decision to remove statutory restrictions on participation in agricultural produce markets midway through the marketing season in 1990 severely hampered the PCU's ability to procure MV seed for distribution, as we saw earlier.

Seed sector development policy

Seed sector development work has been pursued in Zambia with some vigour and much of the necessary legislation is already in place, although there are no plant breeders' rights as yet. In particular, Zambia has a two tier variety release procedure which greatly speeds up the availability of new varieties by allowing the distribution of limited quantities of MV seed whilst field testing is taking place.

However, the lack of a specific, clear overall seed policy is a severe constraint to long-term development: seed issues are handled by individual departments and the Seeds Liaison Committee established in 1985 has no executive powers.

Linkages between organisations

On the positive side, the development of a wide range of well-adapted maize varieties by Zambia's public sector agricultural research institutions meant ZAMSEED has been able to supply MV seed suitable for small farm farming conditions. During the 1980s, this was assisted by the significant donor resources allocated to Zambian agricultural research by Swedish SIDA and British ODA. This is similar to the situation in Malawi, where the national agricultural research system received support from ODA until the mid-1970s and, from the mid-1980s, from USAID, the World Bank, the Rockefeller Foundation and CIMMYT. In contrast, as we shall see in Chapter 7, much of Zimbabwe's variety development work has been done without donor support.

However, there is still a lack of suitable modern varieties in Zambia for non-maize crops. Furthermore, future prospects are not secure as there is no private sector agricultural research as yet and government plant breeding work remains heavily aid-dependent.

In order to speed up variety release ZAMSEED itself took responsibility for all multiplication of breeder seed during the 1980s, at an estimated annual cost to the Company of US$29,000 (Erikson *et al.*, 1989).

The work of the Seed Control and Certification Institute, set up in 1985 with SIDA funding, enabled high seed quality standards to be maintained in Zambia. However, during the 1980s the Institute suffered the same problems as Seed Services in Malawi and in Zimbabwe of lack of managerial and financial autonomy (SCCI is run by the Department of Agricultural Research from its Mount Makulu Central Research Station and still depends on SIDA for half its operating budget). A mid-1980s investigation suggested that up to 80% of SCCI's recurrent costs could be financed through fees payable by ZAMSEED for quality control work, if SCCI were allowed to keep the fees charged (Norrby, 1986). The same investigation concluded that costs could substantially be reduced by using less import-dependent high-tech testing systems. The change to self-financing was approved and by the early 1990s the target of 80% self-financing had been achieved (Moberg, 1994).

Officially the government agricultural extension service is generally considered to provide the necessary amount and type of information on MV seed. However, as we saw earlier, in practice the Zambia seed survey results contradicted this: only 6% of survey farmers said they had received extension advice on MV seed. Importantly, the Zambian extension system distinguishes between different varieties of the same crop in the advice it provides and operates a ladder, or transitional, rather than a package system for MV seed adoption (DanAgro, 1987).

ZAMSEED's linkages with the institutions responsible for secondary seed distribution, fertiliser distribution, credit funding and crop marketing have been less positive. ZAMSEED uses appointed agents to sell seed to large-scale commercial farmers and also has private stockists for vegetable seed sales. However, until the 1990 market liberalisation, it relied entirely on the nine Provincial Co-operative Unions and their 460 affiliated societies for all the secondary distribution of its MV seed to small farmers. The PCUs place confirmed orders with ZAMSEED in the July preceding the start of the selling season together with a 50% down payment on the order. This early down payment was in the past a major advantage for ZAMSEED's cash flow and it provided a significant subsidy for the cost of the expensive small farmer seed services that ZAMSEED provides. However, the Unions were very inefficient operationally. This was in part because they were set up in the early 1980s under the central, government-controlled Zambia Co-operative Federation. Furthermore, as organisations alien to most community structures, they quickly became controlled by local elites as a source of patronage rather than as the rural marketing institutions they were designed to be.

The lack of reliable fertiliser distribution and credit funding systems within Zambia during the 1980s made it very difficult for ZAMSEED to capitalise on potential MV seed sales and to tailor MV seed supply to known demand accurately.

Organisational efficiency

A review of ZAMSEED conducted in 1989 (Erikson *et al.*, 1989) found the company's organisational structure was good and reflected its main functions at that time, namely contract seed growing and bulk seed distribution. Staffing levels were considered to be adequate, except for its marketing functions (one of the main criticisms of ZAMSEED's performance was its low investment in seed marketing). Training was also generally adequate although there had been some 'brain drain' of trained accounts staff to the private sector elsewhere in Zambia. Managerial, administrative, operational and maintenance procedures were satisfactory.

The size of ZAMSEED's operating profits during the 1980s (see Table 6.3) was sometimes criticised. However, whilst it is probably true that some of the company's overhead costs could have been better controlled, it has to be remembered that ZAMSEED also funded a significant amount of agricultural research work and all the primary seed distribution exercise out of these profits. Furthermore, ZAMSEED's heavy reliance on contract growers made production planning difficult and yields were low as there had been little research into seed production techniques suitable for contract growers. Grower area remained constant at 6,000 ha during the 1980s due to the limited attractiveness of seed production for large-scale commercial farmers.

ZAMSEED processing facilities are dispersed at four locations around the country; although this reduces transport costs from grower to factory, it was also considered to reduce overall processing efficiency. Insufficient total processing capacity imposed further constraints on ZAMSEED's operations.

However, in overall terms, ZAMSEED had relatively limited responsibilities during the 1980s. In particular, all secondary seed distribution was done by the PCUs. Also the company was helped by US$138.5 million of support from the Swedish aid programme over the 1980s, covering variety development, ZAMSEED operations and technical assistance.

During the 1980s, a number of important influences on ZAMSEED's efficiency and profitability were external to the company: the range of crops and varieties ZAMSEED was expected to produce was probably too wide to be efficient; the problems with carry-over stocks were largely due to the PCUs overestimating demand; poor uptake of new seed varieties by small farmers was partly because of the lack of PCU marketing and MOA extension for them.

ZAMSEED's structure as a commercially-oriented company made meeting small farmers' seed needs difficult as they are high risk, low profit and difficult to quantify accurately. Furthermore, the price of seed was not regularly directly subsidised in Zambia (although periodically subventions were made by the government to ZAMSEED during the 1980s to avoid seed price increases: in 1987/88, for example, ZAMSEED received US$840,000 for this purpose). This led to conflict as, for example, in 1990 when the sudden liberalisation of agricultural produce marketing left ZAMSEED without the PCUs' normal assistance with its secondary seed distribution exercise. The government pressurised ZAMSEED to provide seed to the PCUs on credit as a temporary solution but, as a commercial company, ZAMSEED could not carry the kind of temporary shortfall this would have created.

Ultimately, it is difficult to measure ZAMSEED's performance in the 1980s against specific targets as few records were kept and neither its own management nor its aid donors had an operational plan for the company. However, according to a 1989 review (Erikson *et al.*, 1989), ZAMSEED's development impact was positive: increased maize seed sales alone were estimated to have contributed up to 10% to national maize production; average annual small farmer incomes were estimated to have increased by ZK250 per household; and the overall national benefits of ZAMSEED's operations were valued at around US$7.2 million annually. A 1986 assessment of the distribution of benefits from ZAMSEED's operations concluded that about 30% went to small farmers, about 17% to large-scale commercial farmers, just over 50% went to food consumers and 2% went to ZAMSEED's shareholders (Norrby, 1986)

6.6 Conclusions

6.6.1 Seed sector performance during the 1980s

Appendix Table 3.2 shows that, of the three countries in this study, Zambia had the lowest formal seed sector margins. Despite this, ZAMSEED profits were amongst the highest in the region. This supports the belief that during the 1980s ZAMSEED was a highly efficient organisation. As in Malawi and Zimbabwe, however, performance in terms of the other primary indicator – national requirement for MV seed – was less good: although the hybrid maize requirement was met, MV seed for other crops was not widely available.

This arose partly from the PCUs' poor performance in delivering MV seed to its depots. But the low level of effective demand for MV seed for non-maize crops also contributed; this arose because low producer prices, insufficient extension advice, and poor access to fertiliser and other complementary inputs conspired to mean that there was little real economic benefit for small farmers from using MV seed for these crops.

A large part of the explanation for this situation lay with the low levels of government investment in agricultural services, including extension and marketing, and in rural infrastructure. Government policy also exacerbated the negative impact of the 1990 market liberalisation: announcing the liberalisation at very short notice, half way through the marketing season, and liberalising only the PCUs' part of the market initially made it very difficult for the market to adjust without disruption.

Thus, it appears that – despite its official status as a parastatal body – ZAMSEED performed efficiently during the 1980s and it was government agricultural sector policy which had the greatest negative impact on performance.

Seed sector policy, on the other hand, was considerably more advanced than in many other African countries, and organisational linkages in the seed chain (i.e. between breeders, SCCI, and ZAMSEED) were also good. Linkages in the seed package (i.e. between ZAMSEED, the PCUs and the agricultural extension service) were much less good and negatively affected the overall performance of the formal seed sector.

6.6.2 Seed sector developments in the 1990s

Organisational change

Encouraged by Zambia's foreign private investment incentives implemented in 1991, Pioneer moved into Zambia in 1991, followed by Cargill and South Africa's Panaar in 1992, and South Africa's Carnia in 1993. Pioneer withdrew within a very short time, because of the introduction of mandatory seed certification, which would have meant it revealing the parent lines of its hybrid maize varieties. Cargill mainly produces MV seed for hybrid maize in Eastern Province, in order to minimise costs by processing the seed in neighbouring Malawi using NSCM's spare capacity.

During the 1990s, ZAMSEED has begun to evolve from a semi-public to a fully private sector organisation; it is investing in its own programme of maize breeding, and it has signed a regional marketing agreement with the seed companies Seed Co-op from Zimbabwe and SEMOK from Mozambique. Following the complete collapse of the PCUs in 1993, ZAMSEED introduced a new seed distribution system, recruiting its own agents to supply retail store-keepers, as well as using direct sales through company-owned outlets and credit organisations. It offers price incentives to its distributors, and promotes its seed lines aggressively using advertising. Although ZAMSEED still has a 90% share of the MV seed market, this is being eroded by Cargill, which deals directly with retail store-keepers, and is thus able to offer bigger margins and more direct marketing support.

The government is supporting ZAMSEED's evolution into a private sector company by selling its 40% share in ZAMSEED: apparently, the government would prefer to sell this share to the Zambia Seed Producers Association, which includes most of ZAMSEED's contract growers. However, some of the multi-national seed companies that have recently entered Zambia may also attempt to buy it.

Ecology and socio-economy

The role of voluntary organisations in the formal seed sector has increased following the 1992 drought, from the limited localised distribution of MV seed for non-maize crops that occurred during the 1980s. However, problems with inadequate planning, late delivery of seed, delivery of poor quality seed, and poor communication with local government agriculture offices have meant that the voluntary organisations' contribution – although well-intentioned – has not been entirely satisfactory.

The drought has also resulted in a policy decision to encourage small farmers to diversify away from maize production to the more drought-tolerant sorghums and millets. Accordingly, from 1993 onwards ZAMSEED has contracted both commercial and small farmers to produce a significantly increased quantity of MV seed for these crops. By 1995, over 200,000 small farmers were being provided with seed for sorghum, millet and other drought-resistant crops under a US$3.2 million donor-funded project.

Macro-economic policy

The MMD government which came to power in 1991 has implemented a wide-reaching programme of economic reform, including the complete removal of subsidies on consumer maize prices, the removal of all restrictions on foreign trade and foreign exchange transactions, the privatisation of many state-owned companies, and reduction in government staff. Despite this, the deficit on the government budget has persisted, prompting the introduction of sales of Treasury Bills to secure short-term funds. This has exacerbated inflationary pressures on the economy, increasing seed companies' costs and economic uncertainties along with those of all other private sector businesses.

SCCI has been particularly badly affected by the combination of continued devaluations and foreign exchange shortages. This has also affected ZAMSEED's contract growers, resulting in zero growth in the grower hectarage in recent years. Government budget cuts have impeded public sector plant breeding work, which has in turn required ZAMSEED and the other private sector seed companies to allocate their own resources to plant breeding and multiplying breeder seed of modern varieties.

Agricultural policy

The liberalisation of agricultural produce marketing that started in 1990 and was completed in 1993 has had a severe knock-on effect on ZAMSEED's seed distribution costs: ZAMSEED can no longer rely on using the PCU network to distribute seed relatively cheaply. The seed survey results suggest that many small farmers have therefore sought seed from other, unofficial, sources or returned to retaining their own seed on-farm and SIDA (1991) found that sales of MV seed for maize fell to just 7,000 tonnes in 1990. The data with which to prove lines of causality are not available but we can assume, given that the varieties currently available in Zambia are known to be popular with small farmers and seed prices have not changed significantly, that this is primarily the result of the market liberalisation.

Seed sector policy

Changes in seed sector policy have been primarily designed to increase private sector participation in the formal seed sector. From 1993, new government released MVs have been licensed to the highest bidder. SCCI's role has also changed to one of minimal regulation. All modern varieties that meet minimum standards are released, and the aim is to disband the Variety Release Committee altogether as soon as possible. In part, this is because the government still lacks independent facilities for variety testing. Although mandatory seed certification was introduced in 1993, seed testing has been made the responsibility of the seed companies themselves, with SCCI carrying out only random testing.

Zambia ratified the international Biodiversity Convention in 1993, and is the home of the SADC regional plant genetic resources centre, but specific project activities to encourage more diverse domestic agriculture have not been implemented as yet.

Linkages between organisations

The main changes in the nature of the relationship between different organisations within the formal seed sector have been in the area of plant breeding. Here, the government has handed over responsibility for the development of new hybrid varieties to the private sector, concentrating itself on new varieties for millet, sorghum and other household food security crops. As we saw earlier, the private sector has also taken on responsibility for the administration of seed certification.

6.6.3 Looking to the future

On the positive side, the increase in the number of seed companies in Zambia during the 1990s is likely to result in an increased commitment of resources to the development, production and distribution of hybrid maize material, because there are high gross margins on the production and distribution of this material. Already 12 new maize hybrids were brought into Zambia in 1992–93 alone. Increasing competition on price and service provided is likely to give small farmers a wide choice of maize MVs, and information acquisition costs are likely to be reduced as a result of the increased advertising and agronomic advice provided by the seed companies. In addition to the domestic market, Zambia's favourable natural resource endowment, experienced contract seed growers, and low labour costs could allow the country to become a regional seed production centre, serving other SADC countries.

On the negative side, the private sector seed companies are unlikely to be able to fulfil both of our two seed sector performance criteria: the supply of MV seed for non-maize crops will probably lose out to the pursuit of organisational efficiency.

The government is increasingly relying on the private sector for carrying out most of the functions of the formal seed sector. In the future, the role of the public sector is likely to devolve to one of monitoring, and the supply of new modern varieties for non-maize crops.

One aspect of government involvement in the formal seed sector which stands out as being very positive is its quick reaction to the changing requirements resulting from the recurrent droughts of the 1990s. Its active promotion of sorghum and millet production may encourage some seed companies to respond by arranging to produce MV seed for these crops and thus go some way towards balancing seed production for maize and non-maize crops (ZAMSEED, as we saw above, is already doing this). The government was the first in the region to respond in this way.

In the long run, Zambia's agricultural market liberalisation may have the advantage of ending formal sector MV seed distribution in the more remote and therefore high cost areas of the country, and encouraging cheaper, locally-based seed production. ZAMSEED's reaction so far to the liberalisation has been to view voluntary organisations more favourably as channels for seed distribution: a number, such as Harvest Help and World Vision, have been buying seed direct from ZAMSEED to distribute in their project areas for some time. However, as yet there has been no official planning for managing this in the changed marketing environment.

There are two good reasons why increasing local community participation in seed production and distribution should have considerable potential for helping to solve Zambia's formal seed sector problems. Firstly, the large number of agro-ecological zones in the country require the production of small quantities of a large number of location-specific varieties: a task that is likely to be cheaper using local level seed production. Secondly, the size of the country and the poor state of the transport infrastructure means that any way of cutting the transport requirement will substantially reduce costs: again, local level production has an advantage here.

However, there is little point in pursuing this or any other approach to improving formal seed sector performance as long as better-performing seed, whether MVs or FVs, remains an irrelevant technology for the majority of small farmers. This would appear to be the case in Zambia as long as producer prices are low and so provide little incentive to increase productivity, and as long as agronomic information about the available modern varieties and their uses is available to only a few farmers.

Chapter 7

The Seed Co-op and Communal Farmers in Zimbabwe: Friends or Foes?

7.1 Introduction

Zimbabwe has a long-established commercially-oriented seed producer cooperative, Seed Co-op, controlled by large-scale commercial farmers. It thus provides an example of the kind of performance that might be expected in the competitive market situation that African economic reform programmes are promoting.

The main Zimbabwe seed survey was carried out in 1989. For the farmer survey, 70 households were interviewed in communal (small farm) farming areas in Natural Regions IV and V (the semi-arid zone) in Midlands and Manicaland Provinces. Households were selected to represent the range of different soil types, farming practices and socio-economic conditions locally. The focus crops were maize, pearl millet, sorghum and groundnuts.

7.2 Background[12]

Zimbabwe's economy suffered badly during the country's liberation struggle prior to Independence in 1980, plus it has many of the structural rigidities common in other African countries. However, its basic physical and economic infrastructure is well developed. Thus, for most of the 1980s, real GDP growth was positive. Nonetheless, there were a number of policy challenges to deal with during this period: controlling inflation and rising unemployment, and balancing the level of government social expenditure considered necessary after Independence against the mounting budget deficit. External debt was also rising. Land reform became

---

[12] The information in this section is taken from Eurostat, 1990 and Lehman, 1990.

a central issue. At this time, Zimbabwe sought to deal with its economic problems primarily through its own economic reform programmes, declining an IMF Agreement because of the perceived social costs of adjustment.

Although agriculture contributes less than 15% of Zimbabwe's GDP, it is very important for employment (accounting for 70% of the active population) and domestic food supplies (in most years, Zimbabwe is self-sufficient in food).

Zimbabwe has a land area of 390,760km^2 – four times as big as Malawi's – but only 7% of this is usable for agriculture. There are three main agro-climatic zones: the lowveld in the North and South, which has a humid tropical climate; the highveld and the Midlands, at altitudes of 900–1,200m; and the Eastern mountains, reaching 2,595m. Both of these latter have a semi-tropical climate. One of the main constraints to agriculture is the wide annual variation in rainfall which makes Zimbabwe prone to recurrent drought.

In 1980 the population was 9 million (i.e. similar in size to Malawi's now), and it has been growing at 3.1% a year since then. Although 27% of the population is urban, shortage of cultivable land remains a problem because of Zimbabwe's inherited agricultural structure, which has meant that only a tiny proportion is available to communal farmers. The area under cultivation increased by more than 75% between 1971 and 1986, and though agricultural production increased by 28% between 1980 and 1988, this did not keep pace with population growth: per capita food production fell by 7% a year over the same period.

7.3 Small Farmers

Prior to Independence, nearly 50% of Zimbabwe's arable land, including the higher potential zones, was reserved for large-scale commercial farmers. Despite an active programme of re-settlement during the 1980s, population densities in the lower potential communal farming areas remain high, with 850,000 households on plots averaging 3ha (MLARR, 1990). This has caused problems of over-cultivation and over-grazing.

Nearly all farmers in the communal (small farm) areas cultivate some maize. The second and third most important crops in area terms are the drought-tolerant small grains (pearl millet and sorghum). These crops are particularly important in the more marginal areas. The fourth most important crop is cotton, which is grown by some 10% of communal farmers. Groundnuts occupy a small proportion of the area, but are grown by more than two-thirds of communal farmers. Sunflower is a cash crop primarily grown in the drier areas as a substitute for maize if the rains are late.

The farming system in the communal areas is determined by the very limited resources available to most farmers: the amount of arable land is small; the quality of land is poor; and rainfall is low and unreliable. The production potential is generally low because of these resource limitations. In addition, poor access to tools and equipment constrains farmers in the communal areas from adopting innovations such as MV seeds (without access to ploughs, cultivators and harrows for timely land preparation and weeding, and access to scotch carts for timely spreading of manure, harvesting, marketing and purchasing inputs, the returns to using MV seed do not outweigh the cost). Nearly 90% of communal farmers have access to hoes and ploughs, but less than one third have access to cultivators, harrows, or scotch carts (MLARR, 1990).

Off-farm employment and income is generally very important for the economy of the communal areas. A farm management survey in the late 1980s (MLARR, 1990) indicated that approximately one third of household income in the communal areas came from off-farm sources.

Farmers in the communal areas make use of a number of strategies to cope with the erratic rainfall and the threat of drought. On the agronomic side, common strategies include staggered planting, intercropping and relay cropping, use of both early and medium maturing varieties, and changes in the cropping pattern (for example to more drought-tolerant crops – such as sunflower or small grains – if rains are delayed or reduced). Socio-economic strategies include migrant labour, buying food from surplus areas, and reliance on food relief.

7.4 The Seed Sector

7.4.1 The formal sector

In 1967 the informal co-operation that existed between government breeders and the various seed producer associations in Zimbabwe was formalised in a Tripartite Agreement for maize. At a later stage, Bipartite Agreements were negotiated for sunflower, wheat, barley, soyabeans, groundnuts and sorghum. The central condition of the Agreements was that all new varieties released by government should be made freely available to the seed associations (the government retained Plant Breeders Rights but licensed the seed associations free of charge to produce seed), in return for the seed associations agreeing their annual production schedule in advance with the government and the Commercial Farmers Union. As it was considered that the seed sector functioned efficiently as a result of these Agreements, they were continued after Independence. The division of labour between the government and private seed sector in Zimbabwe during the 1980s thus left seed multiplication, processing and distribution in private hands, and the government in charge of research, certification, quality and price control.

Seed Co-op – the largest seed company in Zimbabwe – was born out of the merger of the two largest seed associations in 1983. It is a producer co-operative made up of 150 large-scale commercial farmers, which uses appointed wholesalers and retailers to distribute its seed.

Competition between different seed companies did exist in the 1980s for maize, sorghum and sunflower, but not on any significant scale. Savanna Seed was the only company that challenged Seed Co-op in the domestic market, by offering South African released varieties. Savanna Seed did not compete on retail seed prices but offered seed traders a higher mark-up than Seed Co-op. It gained a market share of approximately 5%. One effect of this competition was that Seed Co-op began to be more active in marketing its seed to communal farmers.

For MV seed testing, there are private sector agencies as well as the government Seed Services Unit. Agency status is granted to seed associations which have adequate equipment and experience. Three types of licence are issued by the Unit to the seed industry: an A-licence permits the operation of a seed laboratory; a B-licence permits the packing of MV seed; and a C-licence permits the retailing of MV seed. The A- and B-licence systems function well but the Seed Services Unit is not capable of ensuring that all rural retailers who sell MV seed hold a C-licence. The Unit's effectiveness as a controlling body has been constrained by inadequate resources, particularly lack of transport.

Communal farmers can buy MV seed from local retail stores, from town through a local co-operative or self-help group, or individually direct from urban-based retailers or wholesalers, transporting the seed back to their holding by bus.

Wholesalers of MV seed are all urban-based and located in the provincial capitals, with branches in the district towns. These towns are situated along the main roads, which all run on the ridges through the large-scale commercial farming areas, so the distances from communal areas to towns are commonly relatively large. There were no rural-based wholesalers in Zimbabwe in the 1980s.

Rural retailers are often located in groups at growth points or other rural business centres. The shops are owned by local businessmen and sell a range of products from cigarettes and beer to blankets and kitchenware. The average distance for communal farmers to rural retailers is within reach by foot or donkey-drawn trailer.

7.4.2 The informal sector

Table 7.1 shows survey farmers' responses to questions about source of seed for different crops. It is clear that the use of the informal seed sector for crops other than maize remained very high in the communal areas during the 1980s. As we shall see below, the explanation for this differs from crop to crop.

Table 7.1: Source of seed for communal farmers in Zimbabwe (% of farmers)

Source	Maize	Sorghum	Groundnuts
Farm-saved	2	56	72
Community seed system	13	14	18
Formal seed sector	85	25	10

Source: Zimbabwe Seed Survey, 1989

7.5 Seed Sector Analysis

7.5.1 Primary indicators of performance

National requirement for MV seed

Table 7.2 shows the potential for the use of MV maize seed in the communal areas in Zimbabwe during the 1980s. It is clear that in the decade since Independence, Zimbabwe succeeded in saturating the small farm maize area with MV seed; by the end of the 1980s the vast majority of communal farmers were buying hybrid maize seed annually, and communal farmers accounted for 90% of total maize seed sales.

Comparable data for the other important small farm crops are not available, but coverage of MV seed is known to have been much less – ranging from one third to one half of area sown.

Formal seed sector efficiency

Table 3.2 in Appendix 3 shows Seed Co-op's performance relative to NSCM in Malawi and ZAMSEED in Zambia. From the available evidence, Seed Co-op's performance appears to have been comparatively efficient.

Table 7.3 shows the detailed cost build-up for Seed Co-op single cross hybrid maize seed. Comparing 1990 with 1984 figures, retailer and wholesaler margins remained constant at 15% and 10%, whilst Seed Co-op's overheads increased slightly from 13% to 15%. Seed grower margins, on the other hand, increased substantially. This was the result of the much lower allowances for overhead costs and for finance costs made in the 1990 calculations.

Table 7.2: Potential for MV seed use in Zimbabwe

Crop/Year	1982/83	1983/84	1984/85	1985/86	1986/87	1987/88	1988/89	1989/90	1990/91
Maize									
Cropped area ('000ha)	1,100.00	1,050.00	1,136.00	1,018.00	1,000.00	900.00	920.00	971.00	926.00
Area suitable for MVs	990.00	945.00	1,022.40	916.20	900.00	810.00	828.00	873.90	833.40
MV seed need (tonnes)	24,750.00	23,625.00	25,560.00	22,905.00	22,500.00	20,250.00	20,700.00	21,847.50	20,835.00
MV seed sales (tonnes)	10,550.00	15,050.00	18,150.00	18,300.00	18,850.00	24,550.00	21,400.00	25,500.00	25,000.00
Current market (%)	42.63	63.70	72.01	79.90	83.78	121.23	103.38	114.43	119.99

Notes:

(1) data relate to communal farm areas only.
(2) cropped area from Central Statistics Office Crop Forecasting Committee.
(3) area suitable for modern varieties assumed as 90%.
(4) seed need calculated using sowing rate of 25kg/ha and annual replacement.
(5) seed sales from Seed Co-op.
(6) current market shows percentage of seed need met by current seed sales.

Table 7.3: Cost build-up for single cross hybrid maize seed in Zimbabwe (Z$)

	1984 Z$1 = US$0.79	1990 Z$1 = US$0.41
Per hectare		
Labour	275.00	1,058.85
Foundation seed	41.60	73.00
Fertiliser	187.40	488.42
Crop protection	229.00	341.33
Tractor fuel	128.56	54.00
Irrigation	-	52.00
Packing & storage	18.90	130.00
Insurance	8.16	14.00
Transport	18.69	75.00
Total variable costs	907.31	2,286.60
Overheads	315.99	158.14
Cost of finance	82.29	-
Total costs	1,305.61	2,444.74
Per bag		
Total producer costs	43.52	48.88
Producer price	47.87	80.00
Total costs (inc. factory)	54.83	92.00
Wholesale price	60.31	101.20
Retail price	69.36	116.38

Source: Ministry of Agriculture; Coopers & Lybrand.

Notes: (1) Labour costs include manual labour and supervisory management for crop husbandry, and labour for processing and storage.
      (2) Foundation seed rate = 25kg/ha.
      (3) Tractor fuel = 110 litres.
      (4) Depreciation of capital costs is included in repair and maintenance.
      (5) Land rent is negligible in Zimbabwe.
      (6) Practically all processing of maize seed is done on-farm by the Seed Co-op members. Because processing is decentralised, the only significant cost is packing.
      (7) Part of the storage of seed is done on-farm and seed may be sold and transported directly from the Seed Co-op member to the wholesaler/farmer (although the paperwork is done and permission given by Seed Co-op head office).
      (8) Cost per bag is estimated assuming a seed yield of 30 x 50kg bags per hectare.

7.5.2 Explanatory variables

Crop varieties

During the 1980s, the production and marketed output of maize and cotton in the communal areas increased dramatically, whilst the area occupied by pearl millet declined. These changes in the cropping pattern can partly be explained by the increasing commercialisation of the small farm sector: maize and sorghum production increased because the government supported the marketing network, and modern varieties were made easily available, while this was not the case for pearl millet. Changing food preferences also played a part; as did the fact that, compared with small grains, maize needs less labour, is less susceptible to bird damage and easier to process, and yields better in non-drought years. However, the growth in small-scale maize production had ended by the late 1980s: the evidence suggests that the easy gains from expanding technology and market support were over by this time.

Government policy towards small grains during the 1980s was ambiguous. On the one hand, it wanted to encourage production of small grains by communal farmers as ecologically suitable crops for the drought-prone areas. But on the other, it wanted to discourage wide cultivation of small grains, as they are expensive for the national agricultural marketing parastatal (GMB) to store and from 1984 onwards supply exceeded demand. However, only a small proportion of sorghum produced by communal farmers is sold to GMB: the crop is primarily a subsistence one.

Groundnuts are grown primarily as a subsistence crop, with harvested surplus sold. During the 1980s, surpluses were sold on the local market rather than to GMB, because parallel market prices were at least twice as high as official prices. The main factors limiting groundnut production and official sales in the communal sector were the poor availability of planting material, the fact that groundnuts are a labour-intensive crop and the poor producer price offered by GMB.

Table 7.4 gives details of the modern varieties available for the main small farmer crops in Zimbabwe during the 1980s. For maize, Zimbabwe developed a large number of hybrid varieties suited to a wide range of the country's agro-ecological zones. Although these were first developed for the large-scale commercial sector, they proved suitable for communal farmers as well and there was strong demand for them from this sector.

Not all maize planted during the 1980s by communal farmers was grown from hybrid seed. Local composite maize varieties still existed and were maintained through farmers' mass selection, but they were cultivated on a very small scale only. These so-called farmer varieties derived primarily from earlier releases by DR&SS, the government agricultural research department. In addition, communal farmers did not always buy sufficient hybrid seed so they sometimes added retained second generation hybrid seed to their bought seed. This was typically done for maize cultivated in gardens near the house, but was also

Table 7.4: Seed varieties available in Zimbabwe

Crop	Name of variety	Attributes
Maize	ZS233	White, 161 days
	SR52	White, 158 days
	ZS206	Yellow, 156 days
	ZS107	White, 153 days
	SC601	White, 150 days
	PNR6557	White, 146 days
	PNR6566	Yellow, 145 days
	ZS202	Yellow, 143 days
	SC501	White, 143 days
	R215	White, 142 days
	PNR609	White, 141 days
	ZS232	Yellow, 140 days
	R201	White, 140 days
	PNR6549	White, 140 days
	PNR695	White, 140 days
	PNR482	Yellow, 140 days
	R200	White, 137 days
	PNR617	White, 137 days
	ZS225	White, 135 days
	PNR473	White, 135 days
	PNR6334	Yellow, 130 days
Groundnuts	Natal common	short season
	Valencia R2	short season
	Plover	short season
	Swallow	medium season
	Makulu red	long season
	Egret	long season
	Flamingo	long season
Sorghum	Red Swazi A	open-pollinated, red, short season for brewing
	Serena	open-pollinated, red, medium season for brewing
	Segaolane	open-pollinated, white, medium season
	SV-2	open-pollinated, white, short season
	CD 75	hybrid, medium to long season
	PNR 8544	hybrid, white, short season
	PNR 8369	hybrid, red, short season
	PNR 841	forage sorghum
Pearl millet	PNV 1	short season

Source: Department of Research and Specialist Services

sometimes the case for parts of the main fields.

For groundnuts, the Seed Services Unit conducted a major cleaning exercise and re-released the 1960s variety *Natal Common* in 1986. *Natal Common* is a short season variety and is well suited to low rainfall and sandy soils. However, it was not multiplied and distributed to communal farmers during the 1980s. The seed known as *Spanish* that was sold by GMB during the 1980s was not in fact MV seed at all but a mixture of all groundnuts bought from the communal areas, cleaned and processed and resold. *Plover*, a short season variety that was released by DR&SS in 1982 to replace *Natal Common*, has a higher yield potential than *Natal Common*, is less prone to leaf spot, and has better quality kernels. However, *Plover* too was not multiplied and distributed to communal farmers during this period.

The majority of survey farmers retained groundnut seed rather than purchased it. Retained seed is generally resistant to insect attack, although problems with pests occur in some seasons. The most used variety was *Natal Common*, which has been retained in the communal areas since the original release in the 1960s. The most commonly used purchased groundnut seed in the communal areas is *Spanish,* which – as we saw above – is not strictly speaking a variety.

The potential yield of MV pearl millet varieties is up to six times higher than the 400 kg/ha yields that were being obtained in the communal areas during the 1980s. The modern varieties are also earlier maturing, more drought tolerant than traditional varieties, and shorter in height. However, they are not so well adapted to low input management and to local end uses. Two white sorghum MVs, *SV1* and *SV2,* were released by breeders at DR&SS in 1985 but, due to production problems, *SV2* was not available in substantial quantities until the 1989 season, and *SV1* was not available at all during the 1980s.

According to ENDA, an NGO working in Zimbabwe, there was strong demand among communal farmers for high quality local composite varieties of small grains during the 1980s. A number of farmer varieties of small grains were maintained by communal farmers through mass selection, but not a great deal is known about them. Some information collected by ENDA (ENDA, 1990) shows that many farmer varieties disappeared during the 1980s because of recurrent drought in the communal areas and the expansion of maize and cotton production. Although ENDA maintains these farmer varieties could have been high yielding, in practice they almost certainly yielded less than modern varieties. In fact, part of their popularity must also have stemmed from the limited availability of small grain MV seed in the communal areas at this time, which would otherwise have provided competition for them. However, they are locally adapted to climatic conditions and to small farmers' end uses for them, and they were certainly popular. Out of all the crops grown by communal farmers, it is only the small grains which have this long history of farmer breeding, and are therefore specifically adapted to small farmer conditions.

Seed quantities

Post-Independence commercialisation in the communal areas resulted in a several hundred per cent increase in demand for MV maize seed during the 1980s. The small farmer market for hybrid maize seed was fully served by the end of the decade. But considerably less success was achieved in selling MV seed to the communal sector for other crops, even though appropriate varieties for at least some crops existed and had been released by DR&SS.

Calculated with planting rates of 50kg per hectare, as commonly used by communal farmers (this is half the rate recommended by DR&SS and AGRITEX, the government extension service), the potential demand for MV groundnut seed in the communal sector was around 600 tonnes per year during the 1980s. While the availability of MV seed of the long season groundnut varieties demanded by large scale commercial farmers presented no problems, the availability of good quality short season MV groundnut seed for communal farmers was a serious problem throughout the 1980s. Groundnut seed supply was transferred from Seed Co-op to GMB in 1982. Initially GMB produced MV seed using contract growers, and various other schemes for groundnut seed multiplication and distribution were also tried. However, seed grower prices were too low to attract sufficient production, and recurrent drought wiped out groundnuts in several areas. Therefore GMB gave up producing MV groundnut seed in the late 1980s and simply sold the groundnut crop bought from farmers back to them as standard seed after processing and cleaning the crop (this is the *Spanish* seed that was mentioned earlier).

Potential demand for MV seed for small grains was considerably higher than MV seed sales to the communal areas during the 1980s. Using 1988 data for cultivated area in the communal areas and a planting rate of 12 kg/ha, the potential demand for MV sorghum seed was 2,550 tonnes, compared with Seed Co-op sales of 200 tonnes at this time. Potential demand for MV seed for pearl millet was 2,800 tonnes. But no formal sector production of MV seed for pearl millet took place during the 1980s, so these varieties were not available to communal farmers.

Various problems hindered the production and distribution of MV seed for small grains for the communal areas during the 1980s. Most importantly, there were no clear procedures for the release of breeder seed by DR&SS for multiplication and distribution by the seed industry. Thus, two years passed before Seed Co-op received breeder seed of the sorghum varieties *SV1* and *SV2* from DR&SS and could start initial bulking. In addition, there was little interest in open-pollinated crops within the formal seed sector, and in particular little interest in crops with no clear commercial demand. There was no great interest within the extension service in promoting MV seed for small grains, as no industrial market had been identified and storage costs at GMB were high; moreover AGRITEX extension workers regarded these crops as traditional crops of little extension interest. There was little interest in open-pollinated crops amongst MV seed distributors because they knew there had been no marketing effort by Seed Co-op or AGRITEX. Consequently there was little knowledge about MV seed for sorghum and pearl millet among communal farmers.

Seed quality

Seed quality was not highlighted as an important issue by the Zimbabwe seed survey farmers. In part, this must be a reflection of the high standards demanded by the Seed Co-op of its growers and appointed distributors. In addition, on-farm processing by Seed Co-op members cut costs and reduced delays, as did Seed Co-op's status as a seed certifying agency in its own right.

Access to seed selling points

Before Independence, some hybrid maize seed was available in the communal areas through a government-run 'small pack programme', but the majority of communal farmers did not have access to any MV seed. By the mid 1980s, availability of MV maize seed had improved significantly. A large proportion of hybrid maize seed was sold to communal farmers by rural retailers. For example, Silobela Communal Area, one of the Zimbabwe seed survey areas, is located 80km from the nearest district town, and in this area rural retailers sold about half of the total MV seed sold; the proportion was less in Chiduku Communal Area, the other survey area, because it is closer to the capital city, Harare.

There are a number of reasons for Zimbabwe's success with improving access to hybrid maize seed during the 1980s. First, after Independence the government supplied hybrid maize seed as aid to communal farmers, in a package together with fertiliser and chemicals. Also, the diffusion of hybrid maize seed was part of a government campaign to commercialise agriculture supported by AGRITEX and AFC, the national agricultural credit institution.

However, the marketing of MV seed of crops other than maize was not so successful during the 1980s. On the one hand, trading in MV seed of commercially insignificant crops such as legumes and small grains was not economically attractive to the private sector wholesalers and retailers who were responsible for seed distribution. On the other hand, the demand for MV seed of these crops was low – because of insufficient extension information about their existence, combined with the release of varieties which did not fully take into account the farming conditions facing communal farmers.

By the late 1980s, logistical problems were causing difficulties in the supply of MV seed of all crops. In particular, with increasing spare parts costs many transport operators were not willing to rent out trucks for transport off the tarred roads and into rural areas.

Timeliness of seed delivery

Communal farmers tend not to buy seed until after the first rains have fallen in November. This buying behaviour creates difficulties in delivering MV seed to communal farmers on time: when the first rains have fallen in a given area, all farmers demand hybrid maize seed; but rural retailers operate with low stocks and will not buy large quantities of seed in advance, before they are sure demand will be there.

Despite the logistical problems of distributing seed to marginal areas, hybrid maize seed was generally available to communal farmers in sufficient quantities within a week or two of the onset of the rains during the 1980s. But farmers may not always have been able to choose between different varieties if they bought seed from their local retail store.

Very little MV seed for groundnuts and small grains was available in the communal areas during the 1980s, so the issue of timing does not arise.

Agronomic advice

Government agricultural extension services expanded at a moderate pace during the 1980s and had some success in reaching farmers using a group approach. There was approximately one extension worker per 800 households. However, budget constraints caused a decline in the efficiency of the service towards the end of the decade (Friis-Hansen *et al.*, 1991). Even before this time, there was clearly a lack of extension advice on the availability and use of MV seed for non-maize crops, in part because many of these were perceived by extension workers to be 'traditional' crops and therefore not within the ambit of the extension service.

Part of the reason for the low adoption rate of modern variety seed other than maize is a simple lack of knowledge about its existence among farmers in the communal areas. When farmers do not request the new varieties from retailers, the retailers do not request them from the wholesalers, who in turn do not order seed from the seed companies. AGRITEX could play a valuable role in improving this situation by conducting a campaign to increase awareness of the new varieties of sorghum, pearl millet, and groundnuts.

Seed prices

Under the Tripartite and Bipartite Agreements, the government was responsible for determining MV seed prices. The Ministry of Agriculture and Seed Co-op held talks annually to decide on maximum wholesale and retail seed prices. These talks took seed production costs as their point of departure and allowed a 10% margin, so seed prices were thus directly linked to production costs. This is not a common practice in other countries.

Appendix Table 3.1 shows seed, grain and fertiliser price levels for maize in Zimbabwe during the 1980s. However, seed prices at farm gate level were often considerably higher than the official maximum retail prices.

At this time, there was a statutory ban on the sale of open-pollinated maize varieties, because it was believed that higher-yielding hybrid seed maximised national food security. This increased the cost of maize production considerably for communal farmers: a composite maize could have been a better choice for some poorer farmers. First, they could have retained seed, which would have saved them the trouble of getting hold of seed every year and allowed timely planting using retained seed (late access to purchased maize seed in marginal areas is one of the main causes of late planting). Second, although hybrid maize seed was relatively cheap at this time, the difference in price between hybrid seed and retained seed was between US$9.43 and US$14.15 for the 25kg required to plant one hectare. The money saved by using retained seed would have bought 100–200kg more local maize seed. In marginal areas and under low-input conditions, the yield for hybrid maize is less than one tonne/ha. The hybrid thus had to out-yield the local seed by 10–20% before it would have become economically viable for communal farmers to buy hybrid seed annually.

Nonetheless, after Independence communal farmers had open access to markets for their products for the first time, combined with relatively favourable producer prices paid by GMB, and this initiated a commercialisation process and subsequent demand for hybrid seed.

For groundnuts, although the use of *Plover* MV seed would, from an incremental yield point of view, have been profitable for communal farmers, the price sensitivity for groundnut seed was particularly high. This was because the seed rate is four times that of maize and many farmers were reluctant to buy MV seed before they had been convinced of its advantage. This was rational during the 1980s as *Plover* seed was not being produced, and the only groundnuts available from GMB were the mixed *Spanish* seed. As the cost per ha of using MV groundnut seed was comparable to the fertiliser cost for maize at this time, many communal farmers spent their limited cash on fertiliser rather than risking so much money on seed for which there was a farm-saved substitute.

Where MV seed of small grains was available, retail prices were high as private seed stockists were unwilling to sell seed for which there had been little marketing in the communal areas.

7.5.3 Causal factors

Ecology and socio-economy

Agro-ecological factors Agro-ecological factors affected communal farmers' demand for MV seed in two ways. Firstly, most of the communal areas suffered from low and unreliable rainfall during the 1980s. There was thus a strong need for drought-tolerant crop varieties among communal farmers. However, most large-scale commercial farmers were situated in the higher potential areas, so most agricultural research in the past focused on the problems faced in these areas and neglected the requirements of small farmers. This situation was partly rectified in the first decade after Independence, but few concrete results – in terms of new varieties – were released by DR&SS, and even less actually reached communal farmers.

Secondly, in CDR areas such as Zimbabwe's communal areas, the yield advantage of using MV seed is related to the use of complementary inputs, especially mineral fertiliser. However, the net economic benefit of such a strategy under CDR conditions is doubtful. When there is an early-, mid- or late-season dry spell, communal farmers may lose part or all of their harvest, becoming indebted as a result. It was partly because of this insecurity, that 85% of Zimbabwe's Agricultural Finance Corporation's loan portfolio to communal farmers was in arrears during the 1980s.

Agro-ecological conditions did not adversely affect the production of MV seed in Zimbabwe during the 1980s. This was because virtually all production of MV seed took place on large-scale commercial farms, which are either situated in favourable agro-ecological areas or use supplementary irrigation.

Socio-economic factors In some parts of the communal areas, effective demand for MV seed may be too low to be attractive to the formal sector. This is because, in addition to the small numbers of farmers requiring seed, they may be very dispersed geographically. This low density of demand is linked to the degree of social differentiation in the communal farming sector: the rate of commercialisation varies greatly among farmers and, with it, the ability of communal farmers to meet the management demands required by MV seed in order to get a good yield (use of complementary inputs, ability to plant early and weed satisfactorily, etc.).

The qualitative characteristics of the seed varieties required also vary significantly between different groups of farmers. An example of this is the differing importance of early maturity amongst farmers with and without oxen and ploughs. The delay in planting facing farmers without oxen and ploughs, who often have to wait to rent an ox-team to prepare their fields, causes them to prefer short season varieties compared with farmers with their own oxen. Similar differences in demand derive from variations in household access to labour and land.

Economic conditions also have an effect on the supply of MV seed. Transport infrastructure in the communal areas of Zimbabwe was generally poor during the 1980s. This increased the cost of transporting seed to these areas and thus further reduced the economic viability of selling MV seed in the communal areas. This was especially so when, as was the case during the 1980s, the official maximum retail seed price was strictly enforced: seed prices were pan-territorial, so the allowed mark-up was often not enough to cover the extra transport costs in the more remote areas.

Macro-economic policy

The pressure that the government was under to reduce spending because of its large budget deficit greatly affected the agricultural sector in the 1980s. At this time subsidies to agricultural parastatals accounted for more than one third of the total budget deficit, so the government ordered all parastatals to become more financially independent. This resulted in organisations such as AFC and GMB becoming more restricted in the service that they provided to small farmers.

Budget cuts for DR&SS and the Seed Services Unit were particularly threatening to the long term efficiency of the formal seed sector. The main brunt of the budgetary cuts for the Seed Services Unit during the 1980s was felt in the retailer licensing system, which could no longer provide 100% coverage of all seed retailers. However, the potential negative effects were minimised because Seed Co-op imposed its own strict quality standards on its appointed distributors. During this period, there was a general tendency for an increasing share of plant breeding and quality control functions to be taken over by private seed companies, because budget cuts meant government services fell short of what was needed.

The macro-economic environment also affected MV seed prices directly through tax policy and price regulations. Co-operatives are exempt from tax in Zimbabwe; this gave Seed Co-op an advantage over its competitors, which are all private companies, because Seed Co-op could reduce the retail price at which MV seed is sold, as the seed prices that needed to be paid to growers to provide acceptable returns could be lower than if tax were paid.

The overall shortage of foreign exchange in Zimbabwe during this period affected the purchase of vehicles and spare parts. This had a significant impact on the seed sector as it created a severe shortage of transport in rural areas, which indirectly forced retailers to increase retail prices for MV seed.

Agricultural policy

The provision of credit and extension services was a central element of post-Independence agricultural policy. Credit facilities for communal farmers were rapidly expanded in the early 1980s. The number of loans peaked in 1987, after which numbers declined sharply. The major reason for this decline was poor repayment. By the end of the 1980s, less than 10% of communal farmers received loans to finance their input requirements, such as MV seed.

During the 1980s, produce marketing in Zimbabwe was completely controlled by parastatals, and there was a system of government-set pan-territorial prices. This policy contributed to the success of maize and cotton production, but also contributed to the parastatals' deficits and distorted the market.

Seed sector development policy

During the 1980s the Ministry of Agriculture did not seem to have a definitive policy for the development of the seed industry, nor for monitoring its performance. Assessing how well the formal seed sector was really meeting the seed needs of all categories of farmers was regarded as a technical matter connected primarily with variety development, and was therefore left to DR&SS. However, two areas of seed sector policy did have a very substantial influence on the formal sector's performance.

Firstly, the Tripartite and Bipartite Agreements. The granting of monopoly rights to Seed Co-op to produce seed of government-released varieties, through the Agreements, had mixed results. From the point of view of maize seed production, the Agreements were a success: Zimbabwe was never short of hybrid maize seed. But they were not able to deal with MV seed of non-maize crops so successfully.

Seed Co-op's operations were affected by a number of clauses in the Agreements. One of the most important for the Co-op was the requirement that the Co-op's production schedule be agreed annually by the government and the Commercial Farmers' Union. This stemmed from the government's wish to ensure the adequacy of MV seed supply domestically – and that an appropriate mix of varieties was supplied.

Another part of the Agreements that affected the Co-op's operations was the requirement that the Co-op held reserves of MV seed sufficient to cope with poor years. For maize, this was set at a minimum of 20% of normal annual requirements. Furthermore, because the government did not want national seed stocks ever to run low, the Agreements contained a requirement that Seed Co-op obtained official permission before exporting seed. These requirements did not cause significant problems for the Co-op as it usually kept stocks equivalent to substantially more than 20% of annual domestic requirements, to cope with the large number of requests for seed that are made regularly by other countries in the region.

In the late 1980s, Seed Co-op tried several times to use the Agreements to block Savanna Seed's entry into the Zimbabwe seed market. Seed Co-op was almost entirely unsuccessful in achieving this, however, because there is nothing in the Agreements which directly prohibits competition. In addition, by the end of the 1980s the Ministry of Agriculture was itself starting to favour increased competition in the seed sector.

During the annual review meetings provided for under the Agreements, seed price setting appeared to have been the main recurring issue during the 1980s. Official responsibility lay with the Ministry of Agriculture, but the Ministry of Trade and Commerce became involved in the negotiations in the late 1980s. The Ministry of Trade and Commerce opposed the then system of seed distribution using registered private distributors; from 1990 a new system – which standardised the discounts available at different stages in the seed distribution chain – was introduced. This allowed all wholesalers a maximum mark-up of 10% and all retailers a maximum mark-up of 15%. The consequence of this new system was that wholesalers' earnings were increased on MV seed sales in large packs and correspondingly reduced on sales in small packs (the previous discount structure which differentiated by pack size was discontinued). This is likely to have had a strong negative impact on the demand for MV seed amongst smaller farmers.

Linkages between organisations

The Tripartite and Bipartite Agreements meant that Seed Co-op and DR&SS had a close relationship, as Seed Co-op is the sole user of the new releases from DR&SS of varieties of the crops in the Agreements. However, Seed Co-op acquired the 400ha Rattray Arnold Research Station in 1973 in order to develop its own breeding and variety testing programme, and thereby depend less on the government. It is funded and staffed entirely by Seed Co-op and provides facilities for testing hybrids and other varieties developed by DR&SS under the Tripartite and Bipartite Agreements. More than 4,000 trials were conducted annually at the Station during the 1980s, including approximately half of all DR&SS trials. With the decline in government funding of research in relative terms during the 1980s, private research bodies financed by the large-scale commercial sector, such as the Arnold Rattray Station, increased in importance in Zimbabwe. To an increasing extent, Seed Co-op also provided direct assistance to DR&SS in order to allow it to operate smoothly. This included, for example, managing research trials, helping out with transport, etc.

The relationship between Seed Co-op and Seed Services was likewise close. Seed Co-op is in fact a certifying agency for a number of crops and employed its own seed inspectors, under the formal supervision of Seed Services, which is the certifying authority.

Good co-operation between agricultural extension, research, credit and marketing institutions was clearly very important in contributing to the expansion of maize production in Zimbabwe during the 1980s and the high rates of adoption of hybrid maize seed (a similar level of successful co-operation was not achieved for non-maize crops, however). However, the links between communal farmers and formal agricultural research remained weak or non-existent, even though the post-Independence government was strongly committed to serving small farmers. The re-orientation of formal agricultural research was an important on-going process during the 1980s.

Organisational efficiency

There was a long queue of farmers waiting to become Seed Co-op growers during the 1980s. This supports the evidence in Appendix Table 3.2 that the Co-op gave good returns. The Co-op limited the number of members to ensure economic viability for individual members. New members were chosen from the top of the waiting list, irrespective of their geographical location in the country. This was possible because the Co-op's seed processing and packing facilities were decentralised.

At the beginning of the season, every member was given an equal production quota based on expected sales. If a member did not produce their quota, they might lose their membership of Seed Co-op. All the hybrid maize seed was processed on the farms of Seed Co-op members, all of whom had the equipment to grade it, clean it and treat it.

Members were obliged to sell seed to the Co-op, which in turn ensured that it was distributed. Members were paid only for what they delivered. The Co-op stipulated in its constitution that members had to deliver their summer crop seeds by 15th October to qualify for the first payment. This enabled the Co-op to start distributing to the market on time for the first rains. Growers were paid a premium over the grain price: the retail price for three-way cross hybrid maize seed was about 100% above the grain price and Seed Co-op aimed to pay the seed growers about 85% of this, taking the rest to cover the overhead costs of running the Co-op, including the Co-op's own research farm.

The fact that Seed Co-op is a co-operative, without share-holders wanting an immediate return on investment, contributed to holding down its total seed production costs.

During the 1980s the Seed Co-op had 23 appointed distributors, who handled all seed sales for the Co-op outside its own retail sales outlets in Harare and Chinhoyi. These distributors fell into four groups: national co-operatives; community co-operatives; national wholesalers; and wholesalers with a limited geographical territory. As appointed distributors, they had the sole right to sell seed produced by Seed Co-op. However, to achieve this status, a number of conditions were imposed on them: they were prohibited from selling other companies' seed; they had to ensure given quality standards; and they were obliged to report all instances of seed re-packing by wholesalers and retailers that they came across.

Seed Co-op's appointed distributors sold seed under a discount system dictated by the Co-op. As it had a virtual monopoly on seed sales in Zimbabwe during the 1980s, Seed Co-op was in a very strong position to impose conditions on the distributors. The discount differed between distributors depending on their size and their relation to Seed Co-op. The best discounts were achieved by the Farmers Co-op (the largest marketing co-operative in Zimbabwe, including almost all large-scale commercial farmers) which, given its large market share and status as a national interest group, was in a strong position to negotiate with Seed Co-op. It had wholesale outlets in all the major towns in Zimbabwe.

The smallest discounts were granted to the smaller individual wholesalers, who had to buy from Seed Co-op at a price equivalent to the retail price in Harare. These wholesalers had to negotiate individually with the area-specific distributors for what they wanted to sell from their other branches. The discounts were highest for small packs. The logic behind this was that the 25kg and 50kg bags were often sold in bulk and they involved less work than selling small packs. The high discounts for small packs also reflected a deliberate policy of Seed Co-op of encouraging its seed to be sold as widely as possible.

According to interviews with seed distributors and examination of purchase invoices, the appointed seed distributors charged high mark-ups, of 17–22%, on their retail sales direct to farmers in the provincial and district towns. For MV seed sold through other wholesalers and retailers operating in the same areas, much of this profit margin was passed on, leaving the distributor with a more modest mark-up of 2–5%. The high mark-up for MV seed sold from the appointed distributors' retail outlets was only possible because the distributors had monopolies on MV seed distribution in their area. The price was deliberately held high by the distributors through the establishment of cartels. Wholesalers and retailers who bought seed from the distributors gave informal verbal promises not to sell seed on at less than the retail price set by the distributors. If they did, they were often unable to obtain further supplies of MV seed from the distributors.

Some national wholesalers were opposed to this system and claimed that they could cut the retail seed price in district towns by 5–10% and still make a 10% margin, if they were allowed to operate in a free market, where they could buy seed from Seed Co-op in Harare and arrange their own transport to their branches. The argument against such a liberalisation of MV seed distribution was that the wholesalers would then sell only from the district towns and would not make any effort to get MV seed out to communal farmers in marginal areas. From the available data, it is difficult to judge whether the existing appointed distributors in fact used their high mark-up on retail sales in towns to subsidise the cost of getting MV seed out to the more marginal farmers.

Overall, Seed Co-op's distribution strategy of offering good margins to wholesale distributors appears to have been successful in ensuring the widespread availability of hybrid maize seed in Zimbabwe during the 1980s. Net of subsidy, these margins were highly competitive compared with those in neighbouring countries.

7.6 Conclusions

7.6.1 Seed sector performance during the 1980s

During the 1980s, the formal seed sector in Zimbabwe was relatively efficient compared with the formal seed sector in Malawi and Zambia. In addition to Seed Co-op's internal efficiency, low national wage rates, on-site processing (possible because of the relatively large scale of Seed Co-op's members' seed production operations), and the Co-op's business structure as a member co-operative all kept MV seed production costs relatively low.

And the cost-plus MV seed pricing formula agreed with government guaranteed that Seed Co-op would be able to cover these production costs at all times. The MV seed price-setting formula operating during the 1980s was instrumental in keeping down the cost of MV seed at this time, because seed prices were based on production costs on efficiently run farms, with a margin for the grower and for Seed Co-op totalling no more than 10% in total. These margins were very low compared with those in the formal seed sector elsewhere in Africa, and supported the argument that controlled monopoly systems, like the one operating in Zimbabwe at this time, produce cheaper MV seed than more openly competitive systems.

However, in part Seed Co-op's efficiency was achieved by producing only those MV seed lines for which demand was very strong, because the retailers of Seed Co-op seed avoided stocking less popular MV seed lines. In practice, this meant an emphasis on three-way cross maize seed, to the exclusion of MV seed of other crops suitable for communal farmers, even though useful non-maize modern varieties had been released by DR&SS. Stimulating the market for MV seed for non-maize crops was left to the government agricultural extension service: neither Seed Co-op nor its retailers invested in marketing for these crops to any significant extent.

Thus, as in Malawi, reliance on a relatively commercially-oriented seed sector in Zimbabwe appears to have produced a conflict between the pursuit of efficiency and the optimal distribution of MV seed to small farmers: the two aspects of formal seed sector performance were not pursued in tandem.

From this description of the main factors explaining the performance of the formal seed sector in Zimbabwe, it is clear that organisational linkages were influential in addition to the Seed Co-op's internal organisational efficiency. Three stand out in importance. First, the substantial role played by the expansion of government agricultural produce marketing and fertiliser supply facilities in encouraging commercialisation in the communal sector, and thus strong demand for hybrid maize seed. Second, the lack of emphasis within the government extension service on non-maize crops, which served to dampen the market for MV seed of these crops. And third, the system of panterritorial seed prices that operated during the 1980s. This was intended to favour access to MV seed in the more marginal agricultural areas. In practice, however, this did not happen because, for seed retailers, selling MV seed at the official price in the more remote communal areas was not economically viable. Thus, this system of price control may have made MV seed less widely available that it would otherwise have been.

7.6.2 Seed sector developments in the 1990s

Organisational change

By the early 1990s, the government was beginning to question the value of supporting Seed Co-op's near monopoly in the domestic market for MV seed. Accordingly, a number of other seed organisations were able to increase their presence in the Zimbabwe seed market at this time. Two – Cargill and Pioneer – are international seed companies. Cargill now has about 5% of the seed market in communal areas, mainly in hybrid maize and sunflower seed. Pioneer started to target communal farmers in Natural Region II (the higher-potential areas) in 1993, offering farmers credit to sell MV seed to other farmers. Pioneer has increased its market share significantly as a result of this strategy.

Panaar is a South African company which joined forces with the local companies National Tested Seed and Savanna Seed, to become the market leader in Zimbabwe in MV seed for vegetables. Because Panaar's maize varieties are open-pollinated, they cannot be promoted domestically in Zimbabwe, so for maize seed the company originally concentrated on export sales to Angola and Mozambique. Now, Panaar has about 5% of the domestic maize seed market, mostly in the marginal communal areas. The company has recently formed an alliance with Pacific, an Australian company in the Zeneca (ICI Seeds) group.

Agriseeds is another local company, which supplies MV seed for vegetables and horticultural crops, and open-pollinated maize seed for export.

Most of the new seed companies initially aimed to serve the export market as well as the domestic market for MV seed, in order to avoid Seed Co-op's attempts to block their entry into the domestic market using the Tripartite & Bipartite Agreements. This was possible because there is a substantial donor-financed trade in supplying neighbouring war- and drought-stricken countries, as well as the regular commercial demand for MV seed elsewhere in the region. But now competition to serve the domestic market in the communal areas is becoming increasingly intense, because it accounts for 80% of MV seed sales in Zimbabwe. Some companies are trying to breed widely adaptable, drought tolerant hybrids that have yield potential under low-input conditions; others are competing by bringing in new germplasm with wide environmental adaptability through their international links; and still others are competing by targeting market segments where Seed Co-op is weak (for example, by supplying maize varieties suitable for low rainfall areas).

Despite all this, Seed Co-op has maintained its near monopoly on domestic sales of MV seed, still supplying 70% of the market. It also formed a subsidiary company, Cert Seed International, in 1989 specifically in order to participate in the regional export market, and signed an agreement with the multi-national seed company DeKalb in 1992 to obtain access to DeKalb's technology and marketing channels. Seed Co-op has also formed regional links, with ZAMSEED in Zambia and the seed company SEMOK in Mozambique, in order to share their germplasm and marketing channels.

Voluntary organisations have also become involved in seed production in Zimbabwe, often concentrating on farmers' varieties rather than MVs from the formal sector. For example, the south-based NGO ENDA initiated an Indigenous Seeds Programme in Zimbabwe in 1985, aimed at conserving, testing and multiplying farmers varieties of maize, sorghum and pearl millet. In recent years, it has collected more than 100 different varieties and conducted an on-farm trials programme in six communal areas. In 1988, it began to operate a seed multiplication scheme on a small scale. The idea is to multiply the best of the local composite varieties and distribute them amongst communal farmers. ENDA is also acting as a facilitator for a pilot scheme enabling small farmers to produce MV seed on contract for Seed Co-op. ENDA identifies, trains, and provides technical support to them, whilst Seed Co-op provides foundation seed.

The scale and scope of voluntary organisation activities is very limited compared with that of the private seed companies. However, there is growing interest amongst both government and voluntary organisations in local level seed production as a means to secure more accessible supplies of non-maize seed and farmers' varieties, and there is now a project in Zimbabwe funded by SADC and

German GTZ which aims to promote this in the medium-term future.

Ecology and socio-economy

As elsewhere in the southern African region, Zimbabwe was badly affected by drought in the early 1990s. As well as affecting food production (for example, Zimbabwe achieved only 10% of normal food production in 1992), the droughts have distorted the formal seed sector by the need to distribute fertiliser and MV seed as free drought-relief. By 1994, 50% of fertiliser for the communal areas was distributed as drought relief; given the relatively high cost of domestically-produced and the high tariffs on imported fertiliser, it is likely that fewer farmers would have used fertiliser if this free distribution had not taken place. In 1995, tenders were awarded to domestic seed companies to provide nearly 16,000 tonnes of MV seed for maize, 2000 tonnes for sorghum and millet, and 500 tonnes for groundnuts, for distribution to 1.8 million farmers.

Macro-economic policy

Zimbabwe can compete well on the regional export market for MV seed, because of the country's low wage rates and well-established contract grower base. This explains the importance of exports and regional links to many of the seed companies based in Zimbabwe, particularly during the period when Seed Co-op dominated the domestic market.

Competition in the formal seed sector accelerated in 1990 with the launch of the Economic and Structural Adjustment Programme (ESAP), and thus the removal of a number of the disincentives to foreign private investment in Zimbabwe.

ESAP – which is Zimbabwe's first donor-supported economic reform programme – aims to achieve economic growth of 5% p.a. by 1995 and to create 100,000 jobs annually during this period. This is being achieved by liberalising trade and foreign exchange markets, and removing controls on domestic investment, prices and wages. However, in practice GDP growth has been only 2% over the last 5 years and the early 1990s were characterised by economic recession. Real incomes per head are little different from what they were in 1980 and unemployment has reached major proportions. Inflation at 25% per year, double-digit positive real interest rates and major devaluations have all made the business operating environment very difficult. These economic difficulties have affected the formal seed sector as much as any other sector of the economy.

Agricultural policy

Considerable liberalisation of the agricultural sector has taken place as part of Zimbabwe's economic reform programme. Official agricultural producer prices are now floor prices and the GMB is no longer the sole official purchaser of most agricultural commodities. However, the Board is not yet fully financially independent from government, as originally planned as part of the ESAP.

A Land Acquisition Bill was passed by Parliament in 1992, which would transfer a large proportion of commercial farming land to the communal sector. However, action to implement its provisions awaits discussion of the findings of a land tenure Commission of Inquiry, which were published in 1994.

Seed sector policy

Partly in line with the spirit of the economic reform programme, and partly because recent cuts in agricultural research funding have limited the output of germplasm from the public sector, the government has removed the constraints to private sector plant breeding, and to the import and export of germplasm. From 1994, it has also permitted DR&SS to licence its new varieties to the highest bidder, even though the Tripartite and Bipartite Agreements are still officially in force. The ban on certifying seed of open-pollinated maize varieties has also been relaxed and these varieties are being included in trials and performing well.

It is not clear to outsiders who is currently responsible for setting MV seed prices in Zimbabwe. The 1993 agricultural price liberalisation was assumed to include MV seed prices, but the Tripartite and Bipartite Agreements are still formally in place, so the Seed Co-op still has to agree its prices with government. The other formal sector seed companies appear to decide their seed prices levels themselves (but in practice base them on Seed Co-op prices).

Linkages between organisations

The liberalisation of the formal seed sector in Zimbabwe requires change in the relationship between seed sector organisations in plant breeding, variety testing, seed certification, and other areas. As yet, the pace of this change has not kept up with the pace of liberalisation.

For example, once competing seed companies began to enter the market in Zimbabwe, it was decided to introduce compulsory certification for hybrid maize seed in order to give farmers some degree of consumer protection. However, continued budget pressure has meant that Seed Services lacks the resources to certify the large volumes of seed that have come onto the market, so responsibility has been transferred to private sector agencies.

Also, Zimbabwe still lacks testing facilities to provide farmers with unbiased information on variety performance. The testing carried out for the Variety Release Committee is only for government material.

In general, the development of organisational linkages at the regional level, as we described earlier, has proceeded faster than at the domestic level.

7.6.3 Looking to the future

Macro-economic policy appears to have been the most influential factor explaining the performance of the formal seed sector in Zimbabwe during the 1990s.

Because of the emphasis in macro-economic policy on liberalisation, the reliance on the private sector for the production and distribution of MV seed looks set to continue for the foreseeable future. So far, liberalisation has encouraged an increasing number of seed companies to operate in Zimbabwe. This is producing increased private sector investment in research stations, seed conditioning and marketing facilities, and an increase in the number of maize hybrids on the market. It is also resulting in increased advertising, demonstrations and give-aways, which have reduced farmers' information costs. In addition, new distribution strategies, like selling seed on consignment and on commission, have reduced transactions costs for rural retailers and thus improved timeliness of supply.

The policy decision to rely on commercially-oriented organisations in the formal seed sector in Zimbabwe appears to have produced an efficient seed sector, but one which performs less well in terms of supplying the full range of MV seed required in the communal sector.

In the future, competition between private sector seed companies is likely to intensify as the market for MV maize seed becomes saturated. It may also be the case that the reduction in government support for agricultural produce marketing results in crop diversification, with a consequent reduction in the existing level of demand for hybrid maize seed. This increasing competition is likely to mean that, in addition to MV seed prices, the reputation of the different organisations' seed and the provision of agronomic advice are likely to become major yardsticks by which farmers evaluate different MV seed sources.

The impact of economic reform on the public sector has been to reduce the budgets of government institutions. In the formal seed sector, this is likely to lead to a continuing decline in the government's role; for example, in plant breeding, DR&SS is increasingly concentrating on the development of breeding populations and open-pollinated varieties. In other respects, the government sector has not kept pace with the speed of liberalisation. For example, although they are likely to be dismantled eventually, the Tripartite and Bipartite Agreements are still in place, institutionalising Seed Co-op's dominance in the formal seed sector.

Furthermore, in changing the seed price setting system in 1990, the intention of the Ministry of Trade and Commerce was to improve access to MV seed in remote areas. However, the changes appear to conflict with the way the private seed sector works in practice and therefore actually serve to reduce access to MV seed in some areas. Unless seed price controls are lifted completely, it seems that selective incentives for private traders to encourage them to supply MV seed to communal farmers in remote areas may be needed.

Besides macro-economic policy change, the other factor with a very significant impact on the structure and performance of the formal seed sector during the 1990s has been the recurrent drought. Despite this impact, there has as yet been no formal discussion of how to deal with it: the danger is that free distribution of a limited range of MV seeds will become institutionalised, with all the distortions to the seed sector that this entails.

Chapter 8
Conclusions

The relationship between governments, farmers and seeds in Africa is changing in response to mounting pressure to increase the role of private companies in the formal seed sector, to increase voluntary organisations' participation in seed production and distribution, and to provide varieties that are more appropriate to farmers in CDR areas.

We have seen that farmers in CDR areas have specific needs in terms of crop varieties, seed quantities, seed quality, access to seed, agronomic advice and seed pricing. We have also seen that there are three distinct types of farm household in CDR areas: seed secure households, crisis-prone households, and chronically seed insecure households, and each of these has a different relationship with the formal seed sector.

Taking the evidence presented in this book, what have we learnt about the relationship between governments, farmers, and seeds and how it has changed in response to these pressures?

8.1 Seed Sector Performance During the 1980s

The evidence has shown that during the 1980s there was substantial variation amongst the three case study countries in the size of seed companies' margins over production costs, and not all were positive (see example figures for hybrid maize seed given in Appendix Table 3.2). However, the variation appears to have been related to the price at which governments dictated MV seed should be sold, rather than to the economic efficiency of the seed companies themselves (i.e. growers' costs or factory costs).

Seed distributors had positive margins in Zambia and Zimbabwe, although in Zimbabwe this was only possible because Seed Co-op agreed to wholesale seed at prices lower than full production cost. In Malawi, ADMARC made a loss on its seed distribution activities, in part because it was expected by government to absorb the cost of retailing seed at a considerable subsidy on the wholesale price charged by NSCM. Thus the level of administered seed prices had an important influence on margins in the distribution system, as well as in seed production.

With respect to our other primary indicator of performance – quantity of MV seed used – the experience during the 1980s was not positive. Sales of hybrid maize seed as a proportion of the potential market were high, except in Malawi, but sales of other MV seed came nowhere near to supplying the potential market (see Tables 5.3, 6.2 and 7.2) (the apparent over-use of MV seed for groundnuts in Malawi is an abberation, caused by relative price levels which caused rural Malawians to buy groundnut seed to eat as food).

Out of the six variables identified as having the potential to explain seed sector performance, we found that four clearly contributed to the sub-optimal seed sector performance in the case study countries during the 1980s, as follows.

With respect to crop varieties, the hybrid maizes available in Zambia and Zimbabwe were popular with CDR farmers, but not so those available in Malawi at this time (because of farmers' particular storage and processing practices in that country). Furthermore, only a very limited range of varieties were being produced for other crops in the three countries, and they were not those preferred by CDR farmers.

In terms of quantity of seed supplied, the overall supply of hybrid maize seed by the seed companies was satisfactory in all three countries. However, the supply of the less profitable (but in some situations more popular) single cross hybrids was much lower than that for the three-way cross hybrids, and it was very poor – no MV seed being produced at all in some years – for our other focus crops.

The timeliness of seed delivery was a major problem in all three countries, as was the supply of agronomic advice. In all the case study countries, there were complaints that the coverage of the government agricultural services was poor both in terms of the range of farmers contacted, and the crops and topics covered.

Also, perhaps most damagingly of all, we found that for all crops in all the case study countries – with the single exception of hybrid maize in Zimbabwe – it was not economic for CDR farmers to use MV seed at the prices prevailing in the 1980s. Producer price levels were such that the profit from the incremental yield produced by using MV seed did not compensate for the cost of this seed, at the retail seed prices set by government at that time.

Two of the six variables did not have a negative influence on seed sector performance in Malawi, Zambia and Zimbabwe. Firstly, the quality of the MV seed being supplied appeared to be relatively good – both ex-factory and at point of sale. Secondly, concerning distances travelled to source seed, our evidence contradicts the widespread assumption (see, for example, Gerhart, 1975 based on evidence from Kenya) that there is a strong positive correlation between density of seed delivery points and level of MV seed uptake by CDR farmers.

8.2 The Influence of Organisational Efficiency on Performance

We explained earlier that one of the prevailing hypotheses guiding much seed sector development work in Africa is that the organisational efficiency of the formal sector, i.e. the level of production costs and margins, is the major determinant of seed sector performance.

Our evidence from Malawi, Zambia and Zimbabwe during the 1980s does not support this hypothesis. In fact, the evidence from these three countries suggests that there is a *conflict* between the pursuit of greater organisational efficiency and increased supply of MV seed to CDR farmers.

In terms of overall seed sector performance, two other causal factors were found to be more influential than organisational efficiency. Firstly, government agricultural policy, specifically in relation to the levels set for MV seed and for producer prices. Secondly, the nature of the linkages between organisations in the seed sector, especially those between the seed organisations themselves and the agricultural extension and marketing services.

8.3 Public and Private Sector Efficiency Compared

A second common hypothesis concerning the seed sector is that the best way of increasing its efficiency is to transfer ownership and control from the public sector to the private sector. This arises out of the perception that the private sector is more efficient than the public sector because it is more flexible and responsive to consumers' needs, whereas the public sector is constrained by bureaucracy and policy.

However, our comparison of the parastatals that operated in Malawi and Zambia in the 1980s with the commercial seed sector in Zimbabwe at this time does not support this hypothesis. The parastatal NSCM was relatively efficient even before it was taken over by Cargill in 1988, as was ZAMSEED in Zambia. Although Zimbabwe's private sector Seed Co-op produced seed more cheaply than the corresponding organisations in Malawi and Zambia, the main reason for this appears to have been the economies of scale that the large-scale contract growers were able to achieve, rather than the fact that they were in the private sector. Nonetheless, we must remember that the experience in Malawi and Zambia does not represent the full spectrum of experience in Africa: a number of parastatal seed companies in other countries experienced major problems at this time due to internal organisational inefficiency (for example, TANSEED in Tanzania (see Budden, 1986) and Ghana Seed Company, which ceased operating as a result (*Africa Economic Digest*, October 1989)).

As regards seed distribution, having the private sector involved in MV seed distribution in Zimbabwe did not significantly reduce distribution costs compared with those in Malawi and Zambia, but it did appear to limit the availability of MV seed to one crop, hybrid maize, and to those districts that were relatively accessible by road. Added to this, the point-of-sale cost of MV seed was often considerably higher than the recommended price in the more remote areas, due to the distributors' need to cover their higher overheads in these areas. This may have been possible because in most rural areas, private sector traders enjoy an element of monopoly power because of the poor level of rural infrastructural development. This is of course the case in many other parts of Africa besides Zimbabwe.

Furthermore, comparing between our case studies on other aspects of seed sector performance, the problems of late delivery, small quantities and limited varieties were the same in the private sector seed production and distribution system in Zimbabwe, as in the parastatal systems in the other two countries.

Thus, Zimbabwe's experience suggests that private sector seed organisations can be efficient in the seed production and processing stage of the seed chain, but they are less effective in serving CDR farmers' needs with respect to varieties and retail outlets.

8.4 The Impact of Seed Sector Re-structuring in the 1990s

The restructuring of the seed sector that started to take place in the three case study countries in the late 1980s consisted of two discrete actions. On the one hand, there was the transfer from parastatal to private sector seed activity in the formal sector; on the other, there was the de-regulation of agricultural markets, in the form of ending parastatal marketing authorities' monopsonies and de-controlling prices.

We saw above that the evidence from our examination of the seed sector during the 1980s implies that neither of these actions would, on their own, bring about a significant improvement in performance. The next two sections examine whether or not this implication has been borne out by the 1990s experience to date.

8.4.1 The transfer from public sector to private sector control

In Malawi the transfer of the formal seed sector from parastatal to private sector control appears to have resulted in improved organisational efficiency as NSCM's operating margins increased from 15% to 30%. In Zambia, the results in terms of organisational efficiency are more ambiguous. In both countries, the increase in private sector seed activity also had three other effects. Firstly, it resulted in an increased emphasis on hybrid maize seed production and marketing, compared with the production and marketing of MV seed for other crops. Secondly, it led to significant vertical integration in the formal seed sector, with seed companies buying into plant breeding, quality control and marketing networks as well as taking over seed production. Thirdly, the increase in private sector seed activity produced an increase in the overall level of seed sector investment.

This was most obvious in the advertising and marketing of MV seed. Previously, both NSCM and ZAMSEED had been criticised for their low levels of commitment to marketing their varieties. This increase in seed marketing went some way towards rectifying the low levels that had been a feature under the previous systems of seed sector organisation in the two countries. Thus, the availability of information about MV seed seems to be positively related to the level of competition in the formal seed sector, and should go some way towards reducing the high level of transactions costs that exist in the market for MV seed in Africa. However, it should be noted that the increase in marketing activity relates only to hybrid maize seed: there was no significant increase in marketing activity for MV seed of other crops. Furthermore, the evidence from the three case study countries suggests that private trader involvement in distribution increases, or at least does not reduce, the cost of marketing MV seed. It also tends to create marketing 'gaps' in areas where transport costs are high and/or the overall size of the market for MV seed is unprofitably low.

Thus, for countries in transition to greater private sector involvement in the seed sector, the first obvious result is an increase in organisational efficiency by returning seed organisations' primary focus to their most profitable crops – usually hybrid maize in Africa; and by undertaking more active marketing of their seed. The first of these developments implies a deterioration in the service provided to CDR farmers; the second is of little relevance to CDR farmers as long as economic factors continue to discourage the use of MV seed. This is the case in all three case study countries, as we saw earlier.

Over and above these immediate impacts, the evidence suggests that there are only limited prospects for further expansion of the private seed sector in Africa in the medium-term, for two reasons. First, the cost of transport, and the distances that seed has to be moved on poor roads; and second, the limited prospect of widespread competitive private trader involvement, due to the historical underdevelopment of rural retail trading in many countries.

Kenya's experience is sometimes cited as a replicable example of how to develop private sector MV seed retailing capacity: the Kenya Seed Company aimed to have 'every stockist an extension agent' by providing a range of flexible incentives, including attractive margins, the acceptance of returned stock, and a line of stockist credit (Gerhart, 1975). But these agents were primarily selling hybrid maize seed and it is not clear how this approach could be sufficient in the case of non-maize seed.

Therefore, a different approach may be required, such as the one currently being pursued in The Gambia. Here, the government has handed over nearly all responsibility for multiplication and distribution of MV seed to NGOs and community organisations working at the local level (Cromwell *et al.*, 1993). Or the encouragement of individuals and existing enterprises to become involved in the seed sector, with business and technical advice, loans for capital investments and working capital, and the provision of transport and storage infrastructure.

Thus, in conclusion, it seems that there is no unequivocal difference in the ability of public and private sector seed organisations to produce MV seed efficiently, and so the transfer of the formal seed sector from public sector to private sector control has not had a major positive impact on the overall efficiency of the seed sector. In relation to increasing the quantity of MV used, it seems that the value of structural reforms in the seed sector has been over-stated, because the market failures which constrain the linkages between CDR households and the wider economy, and thus constrain their ability to make use of MV seed, will continue to exist for the foreseeable future.

8.4.2 Market liberalisation

The impact on seed sector performance of the de-regulation of agricultural markets – the other main area of restructuring that affected the seed sector in the 1980s – was much more marked, and at first strongly negative.

De-regulation crippled ZAMSEED's existing distribution network (i.e. the PCUs), reducing ZAMSEED's margins from 18% to 6% within one season (see Table 6.3) and cutting the planting of hybrid maize seed from 100% of the small farm maize area to 70% (see Table 6.2). In Malawi, ADMARC's margins were also negatively affected, and the Corporation faced the awkward situation of being required to compete with private traders physically located inside its own market buildings, although the impact on MV seed use was not marked.

However, in both countries the decline in performance seems to have been a result of the liberalisation *strategy* that was chosen, rather than from the introduction of market competition *per se*. Both ADMARC and the PCUs initially had their monopsony buying powers removed without any changes being made to their seed distribution mandate. It is this partial liberalisation which appears to have caused many of the problems. Other problems were caused by the short time allowed between the announcement of the de-regulation and its implementation.

In the longer term, the evidence presented in the case studies suggests that the main factors explaining the different level of MV seed sales in the countries do not appear to be the inefficiency of the distribution system, but the appropriateness of the available modern varieties to small farmers' conditions, and the level of incentives offered by the seed companies to their distributors.

Proof of the influence of the appropriateness of the varieties on offer is provided by the fact that during the 1980s there was 100% market saturation for hybrid maize in both Zimbabwe and Zambia, even though one country had a private sector seed distribution system and the other a parastatal system, whereas comparing Malawi and Zambia we find that both had parastatal seed distribution systems during the 1980s but Malawi had 6% area coverage of hybrid maize seed and Zambia 100%.

The level of incentives offered to distributors has a significant influence because traders need encouragement before they will become involved in the seed sector, due to the high level of transactions costs. There were no incentives provided to ADMARC in Malawi prior to market liberalisation; indeed, there were significant disincentives because ADMARC was expected to absorb the cost of selling seed to small farmers cheaper than it bought it from NSCM. In both Zambia and Zimbabwe, it was those private sector seed companies that provided substantial innovative support to retailers which increased their market share most rapidly following market liberalisation. The provision of transport infrastructure by government appears to be another critical requirement.

8.5 Suitable Roles for Different Seed Sector Actors

Our assumption that structural and organisational change in the African seed sector needs to be much more fundamental if widespread and long-lasting improvements in performance are to be achieved appears to be validated by the evidence from Malawi, Zambia and Zimbabwe.

In the remainder of this Chapter, we therefore consider the type of changes in seed sector structure and organisation that may be necessary. We start with an examination of the roles that may be appropriate for the different seed sector actors, then we step back and look again at the real role for MV seed in African farming systems, and finally we turn to the other non-organisational changes that may be needed.

8.5.1 The private and public sectors

Thus far, we have argued that a straight transfer of ownership and control of the formal seed sector from the public sector to the private sector is not the most effective means of improving seed sector performance in Africa. This is because there are numerous causes of poor performance in the sector, not all of which can be traced to inefficiencies within the seed organisations themselves.

In many situations, it seems that a less dogmatic approach is likely to be more successful. Thus the critical question with respect to ownership and control in the seed sector is not which particular organisational structure is most appropriate but what blend of organisational alternatives is likely to optimise performance. Therefore the task is to identify the appropriate division of responsibility between government, private sector, voluntary organisations and community seed systems, and the appropriate mix of policy controls and incentives to ensure the efficient and effective operation of these organisations.

In the case study countries, the common trend has been for the private sector – once the seed sector has been opened up to private sector involvement – rapidly to take over variety development and seed production for hybrid maize, and the distribution of MV seed to all profitable market segments (which can include the market in CDR areas, although usually only for hybrid maize seed). The increase in advertising and marketing that accompanies this brings with it the advantage of reducing information costs for farmers using MV seed. Where the private sector has also taken or been given responsibility for seed quality control, the evidence is that it does this satisfactorily, and spot checks are all that are necessary from the statutory authorities.

The cuts in the government budget that form a separate part of the economic reform programme in many African countries have an effect on the role the government can fulfil in the seed sector, restricting the quality control service offered by the statutory authorities, and also restricting the government agricultural marketing network.

Thus, the general trend has been for force of circumstance to leave government with a light supervisory role in the seed sector covering variety release and seed certification, and with responsibility for plant breeding for non-maize crops. For this latter, there is a need for much more – and more accurate – data on CDR farmers' variety preferences for non-maize crops; such data is not yet collected systematically in any of the case study countries. Not all of these functions need to be a drain on the government budget: charges can be made for seed certification services and for licences to use varieties developed by public sector breeders. We saw how, in Zambia, the seed certification authorities have become 80% self-financing since introducing charges for the services they provide.

The experience in Malawi, Zambia and Zimbabwe indicates that for private sector involvement really to take off, the government must also be prepared to relinquish control in other areas. If this is not done, private sector initiative will be stifled (by, for example, insisting on independent characterisation for all private sector varieties) or the controls will not be implementable in practice (as was the case in Zimbabwe, for example, when attempts were made to stipulate the mark-ups private sector seed traders could charge on the MV seed that they sold).

Probably of greatest importance is the need to provide an enabling policy environment. One example of this would be ending the practice of limiting the number of varieties that are released. Neither is it appropriate for government to try to participate directly in the seed market, as experience with doing this in Malawi and Zambia suggests that it is inefficient and negatively affected by policy changes and budget cuts. However, the evidence suggests that it is helpful if the government can provide agricultural extension on on-farm selection and storage for non-maize seed.

One area where government *does* need to impose conditions on the private sector is the maintenance of adequate seed reserves to meet fluctuating demand. Because of the complex, diverse and risky environments in which they operate, CDR farmers' demand for MV seed fluctuates much more widely, in response to climatic variation, than does commercial farmers' demand, which private sector seed companies are more used to serving.

8.5.2 Voluntary organisations

Voluntary organisations have an important role to play in the seed sector[13]. Functions that they can usefully perform include organising seed production for open-pollinated maize (as long as the use of open-pollinated varieties is officially permitted), cleaning and treating non-maize seed, and demonstrating new material that might be useful to farmers for its non-yield attributes (for example, to fit particular agro-ecological niches, taste preferences, storage conditions or processing techniques).

However, in order to do this successfully, voluntary organisations must have skilled seed technology expertise available. They must also build on existing community seed systems, albeit they may need to make them more egalitarian, rather than setting up parallel structures. Also, they must recognise that they are unlikely to cover the costs of their seed activity.

The evidence from the case study countries shows that two assumptions that voluntary organisations commonly make are often not valid. Firstly, the assumption that seed production can be an income-generating activity for small farmers, and that any small farmer can benefit from this: in practice, seed production is rarely economic for small farmers, and only the better-resourced farmers will be able to be involved. Secondly, the assumption that post-emergency distribution of MV seed has no disadvantages is not true: it can be a major contributor to the erosion of local plant genetic diversity, amongst other things.

8.5.3 The informal seed sector

As we have seen throughout this book, much of the debate concerning seed sector performance focuses on the formal sector, but it is important to remember that the formal sector is not always the preferred source of seed for CDR farmers. In earlier Chapters, we saw that between 70% and 90% of seed for non-maize crops is sourced by CDR farmers through the informal seed sector, i.e. from farm-saved seed and through the community seed system.

Farm-saved seed

The evidence from our three case study countries about farmers' success in maintaining seed on-farm was mixed. Contrary to other evidence published elsewhere, our seed surveys suggested that farmers' knowledge of seed saving was often low; their efforts were beset by problems of cross-pollination for maize, and farmers did not in fact treat the storage and care of seed any different to that of grain. On the other hand, a number of FVs and derivations from past releases of MVs were clearly being maintained successfully on-farm over many

---

[13] Cromwell *et al.*, 1993 gives further information.

years. Furthermore, although much evidence has been published of farmers' skills as plant breeders, storers and selectors of seed on-farm, there are high temperatures and relative humidities over much of Africa and these make saving seed on-farm difficult.

Thus, as a recent survey concluded (Wright *et al.*, 1994), existing seed care practices for traditional crops could be improved in many African farming systems, with the effect of increasing the quantity of seed saved and also the range of crops and varieties. For example, for certain crops in certain environments, the FVs already in use are well adapted to local conditions and it is relatively easy to maintain varietal purity on-farm, but maintaining physical quality (seed health, germination capacity, etc.) is difficult, due to high temperatures and relative humidities. In this situation, the main requirement for improving seed sector performance is for help with improving the physical quality of existing varieties rather than the introduction of new varieties such as MVs. ACORD's seed bank programme in Eastern Sudan found that having introduced simple techniques for improving the physiological quality of seed, local varieties performed as well as, if not better than, the modern varieties (Renton, *pers. comm.*).

But improvements in on-farm seed care practices are particularly important where new crops and varieties are being introduced, whether this is for increased productivity, or for diversification or in response to climatic change. This is the case, for example, with beans in the Great Lakes Region of East Africa, where physical quality is maintained to a high standard on-farm and the need now is for new genetic material (Sperling *et al.*, 1992).

Such improvements include:

- *Production practices*: where increasing the quantity of seed produced is important, planting seed crops at lower densities than grain crops can increase the final seed yield. Keeping seed plots separate from food plots can reinforce the distinction in farmers' minds that seed plots need slightly more attention for maximum results. For seed plots of crops prone to pest and disease attack when grown in pure stand, for example beans, it may be worthwhile to introduce special pest and disease control practices, either biological methods or chemical sprays.
- *Varietal purity*: for self-pollinated crops, simple guidelines for how to prevent mixing of seed of different varieties during harvest, on drying floors and in storage can be helpful; for cross-pollinated crops, training in how to isolate seed plots of different varieties either by distance or in time (for example, by staggered planting) can be useful; as can training in how to rogue off-types and weeds in crop stands as well as diseased plants. Encouraging in-field selection of seed during the growing season, rather than selection after harvest, allows farmers to select for characteristics such as plant type as well as grain size and colour.

- *Germination*: locally-adapted training in the best time to harvest in order to maximise germination (this may involve early harvesting, before the rest of the crop, or late harvesting after rains have finished, depending on the area and variety), in rapid drying techniques and in subsequent storage can be helpful. In some situations, it may be relevant to introduce simple pre-planting germination tests and methods for breaking dormancy in recalcitrant seeds.
- *Seed health*: improvements that can be useful include encouraging the rotation of plots used for seed production in order to minimise the build-up of pests and diseases; and training in the recognition and removal of diseased grains, in simple insect control techniques in storage, and in simple seed health tests (for example, floating seeds in water to identify light-weight, non-viable seeds).

Community seed system

Sourcing seed through the community seed system offers clear advantages to CDR farmers because small quantities can be obtained, seed is readily available at the time that it is required for planting, and payment for the seed can be made by a variety of other means besides cash. In addition, the community seed system can be a good source of seed for less common varieties. However, nowadays the availability of these varieties is drying up in many regions, as a result of drought and the resulting post-emergency seed distribution, which usually consists only of MV seed.

But it is important to remember that the community seed system is *not* always the preferred source, for a variety of reasons. Firstly, there is often considerable hoarding of seed, which makes access difficult. Secondly, access to seed through the community system can be less egalitarian, both in terms of prices charged and physical accessibility to all social groups, than access through the formal sector. Finally, sometimes the seed available through the community system is of poor quality (hence, for example, the preference for neighbours' seed over seed from local markets for groundnuts in Malawi).

8.6 The Role of MV Seed in CDR Farming Systems

It is widely known that using MV seed has the potential to increase crop yields, and for this reason the use of MV seed by all types of farmers – whether in the commercial farming zones or in the complex, diverse and risky areas – is widely promoted by governments in Africa. However, the experience in our three case study countries has shown that, for non-maize crops, the incremental yield obtained from using MV seed under CDR management conditions can be negligible. This is because many farmers in CDR areas are unable to carry out husbandry tasks such as weeding and fertilising on time and technically optimally, due to shortage of labour, competing demand for resources from the numerous crops in their complex farming systems, and shortage of capital resources. Trials in other African countries have reached the same conclusion: see, for example, Allan, 1968 in relation to Kenya.

Not only is the incremental yield from using MV seed often low for CDR farmers: our evidence has also shown that for many crops farmers in CDR areas require attributes other than high yield potential (for example, storability, taste, etc), in order to fit the crop into their complex cropping patterns and end uses. This contrasts with the conclusions usually drawn by varietal adoption studies; see, for example, a recent study of rice varietal development for developing countries by Evenson and David, 1993.

Therefore both these factors limit the attractiveness to farmers in CDR areas of the currently available MV seed for non-maize crops.

Thus, for MV seed to be useful in CDR farming systems, is has to be adapted specifically to the needs and constraints facing farmers in these systems. As we explain in Appendix 1, in many African countries technical and economic factors combine in such a way that, in contrast to other crops, MV seed for hybrid maize *is* well-adapted to CDR farmers' needs. Therefore, there is often a considerably greater role for MV seed for hybrid maize in CDR farming systems in Africa than there is for MV seed of other crops. Furthermore, the utility of the specific modern varieties on offer would appear to be one of the main factors explaining the differential uptake of MV seed for hybrid maize in Malawi, Zambia and Zimbabwe (compare the low uptake of hybrid maize in Malawi, until *MH17* and *MH18* were produced, with the widespread adoption of the *MM600* and *R200* series varieties in CDR areas in Zambia and Zimbabwe).

Is there a conflict between productivity and diversity?

Together with most other African countries, all three case study countries have ratified the international Convention on Biological Diversity. This commits signatories to promoting the use of a wide range of crops and varieties in domestic agriculture, and to supporting international efforts to do so. However, we saw in Section 2.1 of Chapter 2 that the formal seed sector tends to develop and promote a limited number of high potential yield MVs at any one point in time. Is there, therefore, a conflict between increasing productivity by using MV seed and supporting plant genetic diversity in agriculture?

The evidence presented in this book suggests that there is, but that this conflict is more the result of constraints on the supply side (the formal sector finds it difficult to produce large numbers of MVs composed of material from a diverse genetic pool), rather than demand-side constraints on farmers' willingness to plant many crops and varieties. Work in Ethiopia, Kenya, Sierra Leone and Rwanda (see Section 2.4.1), as well as the three case studies, confirms that farmers in CDR areas are keen to maintain and utilise a diverse range of crops and varieties.

On-going work in Zimbabwe (see van Oosterhout, 1995) is investigating the extent to which farmers' attitudes towards plant genetic diversity vary depending on whether the crop is grown for sale or for domestic use. This work will provide further understanding of the relationship between productivity and diversity. In the meantime, the evidence from our case studies suggests that a conflict between the two exists only for crops grown mainly for sale. In these three countries, this is primarily hybrid maize; for local maize and non-maize crops, farmers want to be able to plant a wide range of varieties, including FVs as well as MVs.

How the formal seed sector can support diversity

Although there can be conflict between the output of the formal seed sector and the maintenance of plant genetic diversity in agriculture, there are also a number of ways in which the formal sector can support diversity.

With respect to formal sector plant breeding, were governments to end the practice of limiting the number of varieties passed by national Variety Release Committees for multiplication and distribution, and to end the use of Recommended Lists, this would do much to encourage the availability of a more diverse range of MVs. As would national governments' use of more flexible *sui generis* systems of Plant Breeders' Rights, rather than signing up to the prevailing but inflexible Union for the Protection of Varieties (UPOV) system[14].

Flexibility in seed production itself can also help diversity. Whilst the private sector is willing and able to take responsibility for the production and distribution of MV seed for hybrid maize, production of FVs and MV seed for non-maize crops also needs to be assured. As we saw earlier, it is unrealistic to expect the private sector to distribute this wider range of varieties, so voluntary organisations can play an important role. It may also be useful to provide training in saving seed on-farm, so that farmers can independently maintain existing levels of diversity in the farming system.

One situation in which particular care needs to be taken not to jeopardise plant genetic diversity in agriculture is that of post-emergency seed distribution. When the immediate priority is to replace planting material lost through drought or war in time for the up-coming agricultural season, it is easy for little attention to be paid to the origin and characteristics of the varieties being provided. Unfortunately, this can have a major detrimental impact, unless some effort is made at the time or subsequently to help farmers re-stock with seed of as many of their local crops and varieties as possible, and not only with MV seed.

However, all these strategies will only work to support plant genetic diversity in agriculture if there is no economic penalty attached to maintaining diversity. In many countries in Africa, the strong government promotion of hybrid maize, through price support, input subsidies, etc, creates just such a penalty and can

---

[14] For more information on the impact of regulatory frameworks on the seed sector, see Tripp, 1995.

make it very difficult for seed suppliers and farmers alike to work for a more diverse agriculture.

8.7 Other Factors Influencing Seed Sector Performance

We have seen in this book how the causes of poor performance in the seed sector can be grouped into four sets of factors: ecology and socio-economy; national policy; linkages between organisations; and organisational efficiency. According to the experience of the three case study countries, real improvement in the seed services provided to farmers in CDR areas in Africa requires much more than simply restructuring the formal seed sector to try to improve organisational efficiency.

In this Section, we therefore discuss the policy changes that may be needed to deal with the other three sets of factors causing poor performance. Of all these factors, the evidence from the country case studies suggests that national policies and linkages between organisations are the two with the greatest influence on seed sector performance.

8.7.1 Agro-ecology

One clear lesson from the evidence presented in this book is that CDR farming systems are characterised by the existence of many ecological micro-niches. Farmers in these areas secure their livelihoods by exploiting the complexity and diversity of the ecological system, and need varieties that help them to do this. The policy implication of this is that plant breeding and variety evaluation systems must continue to change in favour of allowing farmers access to a wider range of material, in addition to conventional MVs.

One ecological issue that is currently particularly important in southern Africa, but is also influential elsewhere in the continent, is drought. Some observers suggest that the recurrent southern African droughts of the 1980s and 1990s are the result of a long-term decline in rainfall and, as maize is not a suitable crop for these drier conditions, other more drought-tolerant crops should be promoted. In the southern Africa context, this means small grains (sorghum, millets) in particular. Creating this change in the cropping pattern requires governments to accept a policy change from the traditional heavy promotion of maize, and requires seed companies to comply with it (we saw in Chapter 3 that seed companies have a vested interest in promoting MV seed for hybrid maize as this is one of their most profitable lines).

These effects of drought itself and the effects of drought relief are two separate issues and must be treated as such. The content and structure of drought relief operations can have their own very significant impact on the seed sector, entirely separately from the impact of drought itself. For example, in the case study countries the common practice of distributing only MV seed (and usually only hybrid maize seed) in drought relief packages has artificially inflated the use of MV seed, at the cost of some traditional FVs falling out of use. This has potentially serious longer-term consequences for the security of the livelihoods of farmers receiving these packages.

8.7.2 Socio-economy

The need for the varieties on offer to fit the socio-economic context of farmers in CDR areas emerges as being an essential requirement that is often over-looked.

For maize, the three case study countries have achieved this: Zimbabwe has the *R200* series; Zambia has replaced the old *SR52* with the new *MM600* series; and Malawi has developed *MH17* and *MH18* to meet the specific on-farm storage requirements of CDR farmers in Malawi. But for other crops, MV seed still remains little used by CDR farmers because it does not yield under CDR farmers' management conditions, and does not have the non-yield attributes which are important for these non-cash crops. The requirement is therefore to make material available that does not require significant extra labour, and satisfies farmers' preferences concerning pest resistance, cooking qualities, by-products, etc.

8.7.3 Macro-economic policy

Because of the strength and complexity of the seed sector's upstream and downstream linkages, as shown in Diagram 3.1, components of macro-economic policy have a very significant influence on the performance of the sector.

Some of the more influential components include the level of trade tariffs, the prices set for variables such as labour inputs and fuel, and the level of government expenditure on transport infrastructure.

Based on the evidence from Malawi, Zambia and Zimbabwe, it seems that the net impact of macro-economic reform on the formal seed sector appears on balance to have been an *increase* in operating costs. This is because the downward distortions that existed pre-reform on many of the macro-economic variables that are important in the formal seed sector (the exchange rate, the interest rate, etc) have been removed. The removal of these distortions affects not only the MV seed producing and distributing organisations but also the linked institutions in the seed 'chain': many public sector plant breeding institutions, for example, have been negatively affected by the cuts in the government budget that form part of the reform programmes.

This negative impact has been exacerbated by the fact that many of the reforms that have been implemented to date have substantially increased costs, whilst other reforms which might have had an off-setting impact, such as those to control domestic inflation, have not yet taken effect.

Looking ahead to the 1990s and beyond, the evidence suggests that seed sector performance will be helped by the implementation of the macro-economic reforms with an off-setting impact on costs, and by the introduction of policy incentives for private sector investment. Where these have already been introduced, for example in Zambia and Zimbabwe, they have had a clearly positive impact on the level of private sector investment in the seed sector. The evidence from the country studies suggests that this will be helpful in overcoming the lack of competition in the seed sector which has, to date, limited the benefits from transferring ownership and control from the public to the private sector.

8.7.4 Agricultural policy

In the same way that the strength of the seed sector's upstream and downstream linkages mean that macro-economic policy has a significant influence on the performance of the sector, so too do they mean that agricultural policy is very influential.

Historically, the orientation of agricultural policy in Malawi, Zambia and Zimbabwe towards encouraging maize production led to farmers prioritising this crop and investing fewer resources in the production of other crops. Without sufficient labour and fertiliser, there was therefore no rationale for using MV seed to plant these other crops. Allocating scarce cash to other purchases (for example, fertiliser for maize) generated better real returns for farmers in CDR areas.

During the 1980s, the erosion of the value of official producer prices in real terms, compared with MV seed retail prices, and the maintenance of consumer grain prices at low real levels (see Appendix Table 3.1) had a further depressing effect on the incentive to use MV seed.

Because the first rounds of economic reform in the agricultural sector concentrated on restoring producer prices for export crops, these first reforms had little impact on the incentive for CDR farmers to buy MV seed. Neither did farmers in CDR areas benefit when attention subsequently turned to reforming the agricultural marketing parastatals: the previous policy of maintaining pan-seasonal and pan-territorial agricultural prices at parastatal depots had provided these farmers with an implicit subsidy and this was now removed.

At the same time, it was not possible to ameliorate the negative impact of the producer price structure on MV seed use by keeping the retail price of MV seed low, because this would have made formal sector MV seed production and distribution uneconomic. As we saw earlier, the effect of the wider macro-economic reform initiatives being pursued at the same time was to increase the sector's operating costs. Assuming the organisations were not making excess profits before, this increase had to be passed on in the form of higher prices to MV seed users (given that increased subsidies from government were highly unlikely). This further depressed the returns to using MV seed.

This clearly illustrates the difficulty with achieving efficient, unsubsidised MV seed production and distribution without also removing controls on producer prices.

Thus, there is a need for agricultural policy decisions to take into account the direct effects on MV seed uptake. The general difficulty of creating a market-driven seed sector in economies with controlled agricultural prices has been illustrated clearly by the experience of all three countries. Increased uptake of

MV seed remains dependent on achieving *real* increases in producer prices for food crops, and on increasing the productivity of the available varieties under CDR management conditions. This is clearly demonstrated by the experience of Zimbabwe, where the maintenance of agricultural producer prices at relatively high levels has contributed to the substantial increase in the use of MV seed for hybrid maize in the communal areas since Independence.

In Zambia, there is already evidence of crop diversification – and thus the potential for increased use of MV seed for non-maize crops – in response to increased fertiliser prices and increased producer prices for other crops, implemented as part of the agricultural sector reform programme.

A final important point to remember as regards the impact of agricultural policy on seed sector performance is that, as we saw earlier, according to the experience of the case study countries, there is only one thing worse for seed services to CDR farmers than agricultural sector restructuring and that is selective restructuring. For example, removing statutory controls on market participation without ending price de-control often provides no real incentive to private traders and results in significant reductions in the overall coverage and equity of the national agricultural marketing system, with knock-on effects on MV seed supply. The case study country experience suggests that it is essential to implement a comprehensive reform that deals with all the key market variables uniformly.

8.7.5 Seed sector policy

Of the three case study countries, Zimbabwe has historically had the most regulated seed sector, through the country's Tripartite and Bipartite Agreements. These agreements are unique to Zimbabwe, the original aim behind them being to create a state-controlled seed monopoly to serve the large-scale commercial farming sector whilst securing its efficiency by leaving production in private hands. This is somewhat contrary to the conventional image of the Zimbabwe seed sector as being one of the most market-oriented in Africa. The protected access to seed varieties produced by the public sector that the Agreements gave to the Seed Co-op made it difficult for other seed companies to compete in the seed sector in Zimbabwe.

In Malawi and Zambia, there has been a big change in the way that seed sector policy is handled during the period under review in this book. At first, most of the variables influencing seed sector performance were determined by non-seed concerns, producing a disjuncture between agricultural producer prices and MV seed prices, and seed sector policy was generally reactive in nature. However, there is clear evidence that in recent years there has been an awakening to the need to make some special seed sector policies. In particular, these policies include attracting private sector participation through investment incentives, liberalising variety release procedures (for example, Zambia's use of a two-tier variety release system), and implementation of intellectual property protection for plant breeders through Plant Breeders' Rights.

Looking to the future, seed sector policy could support improved performance in the sector in a number of ways that provide incentives and support services. Changes that could be implemented immediately include:

- *Seed sector development policy*: all countries are now receptive to the idea of reducing government control of seed production and distribution, but so far most are thinking only in terms of transferring public sector facilities to the private sector. Refinement of incentive structures to include partial privatisation of the seed sector would be helpful, promoting private sector organisation and management only where it is likely to be beneficial in overall terms – for example, in the production of MV seed for hybrid maize. Incentives could then encourage other organisations to take on responsibilities where they have a comparative advantage. For example, voluntary organisations could become involved in farmer training, the informal seed sector in local-level seed production for some crops, and the public sector could continue supervision of seed quality control.
- *Government expenditure*: as part of this revision of incentive structures, there would need to be a transfer of a proportion of seed sector funding to local-level support for voluntary agencies and farmer training.
- *Regulatory frameworks*: at the same time, support services would need to be re-structured. As regards regulatory frameworks, one obvious revision would be to modify the seed quality control system so that seed produced within the informal sector could be recognised as 'seed'. This would improve the incentives to informal sector seed production by enabling producers to charge a margin on this material.
- *Farmer training*: linked to this, it might be helpful if the agricultural extension service placed greater emphasis on farmer training in on-farm seed selection and maintenance techniques, in order to enable them to participate in informal sector seed production.

8.7.6 Linkages between organisations

The functional domestic links (i.e. between organisations involved in plant breeding, seed production and seed processing) that have traditionally been important in the seed sector (remember Diagram 3.1), are likely to become much less important in the future. This is because of the vertical integration that is taking place in the sector, with seed companies buying into upstream plant breeding and downstream distribution networks, so that many functions are performed by a single organisation. Agronomic advice is one function where vertical integration is likely to be extremely beneficial – farmers' poor access to agronomic advice about seed has been a significant constraint on seed sector performance in the past. However, it should be remembered that most seed companies are investing in advertising and marketing for MV seed for hybrid maize alone, not for all crops.

As domestic links decline in importance, so will regional co-operation and trade become more important – in both plant breeding, and exports and imports of MV seed. Regional links need to be facilitated in order to create genuinely competitive markets for MV seed and to allow each seed company to serve a sufficiently large market to be profitable. The small size of many domestic markets for MV seed in Africa, which effectively prevents the establishment of more than one seed company, is a major barrier to more effective domestic competition at present. There is already at least one example of successful regional linkages in operation in our case study countries: Cargill is producing MV seed for hybrid maize in Eastern Zambia, where field costs are relatively low, but processing it over the border at its NSCM plant in Malawi, where there is spare capacity.

The new nature of linkages between organisations in the seed sector requires new linkage mechanisms. Coordination of complementary private sector, government, voluntary agency, and informal sector activities will become more important, as the range of players in the seed sector increases in response to the twin opportunities of economic reform and the push for more participatory development.

8.8 Closing Remarks

It is useful to examine the scope for privatisation in agricultural markets in developing countries in the context of the seed sector as it highlights many of the most important issues involved in the current debate about the relationship between governments and farmers in Africa: the nature of market failure; the shortcomings of complete reliance on the private sector; the potential contribution of a reformed public sector; and the extent to which structure and ownership are the major constraints to improved performance and therefore the extent to which privatisation or market liberalisation can bring about an improvement.

From the evidence presented in this book, we have seen that one of the most important findings for the organisation of the seed sector is that a different mix of organisations is likely to be required in different specific situations, depending on the precise interplay of structural and technical factors.

References

ACTIONAID (1993) *Malawi Drought Relief Seed Distribution Project: Project Evaluation.* ActionAid, London.

Africa Economic Digest (1989) Ghana Seed Company closes. *Africa Economic Digest* 10(38).

Agro-Economic Survey (1987) A production cost survey of smallholder farmers in Malawi. *AES Report* No.55. Agro-Economic Survey, Ministry of Agriculture, Lilongwe.

Ahmed, I. and Ruttan, V.W. (eds) (1988) *Generation and Diffusion of Agricultural Innovations: the Role of Institutional Factors.* Gower, UK.

Ali, M. and Byerlee, D. (1991) Economic efficiency of small farmers in a changing world: A survey of the evidence. *Journal of International Development* 3(1), 1–27.

Allan, A.Y. (1968) Maize diamonds: some valuable results from the district husbandry trials in 1966. *The Kenya Farmer*, January.

Arndt, T., Dalrymple, D.G. and Ruttan, V.W. (eds) (1977) *Resource Allocation and Productivity in National and International Agricultural Research.* University of Minnesota Press, Minneapolis.

Arnon, I. (1989) *Agricultural Research and Technology Transfer.* Elsevier, London and New York.

ARPT (1991) *National Seed Availability Study: Seed Problems, Practices and Requirements Among Small-Scale Farmers in Zambia.* Adaptive Research Planning Team, Ministry of Agriculture, Lusaka, Zambia.

Ashworth, V.A. (1990) *Agricultural Technology and the Communal Farm Sector.* Zimbabwe Agricultural Sector Memorandum. World Bank, Washington D.C.

Barton, L.V. (1961) *Seed Preservation and Longevity.* Leonard Hill, London.

Bentley, F., Griffiths, R. and Reusche, G. (1986) *Improved Seed Systems for Africa.* Report prepared for Winrock International, USA.

Berg, T. (1992) Indigenous knowledge and plant breeding in Tigray, Ethiopia. *Forum For Development Studies* No.1.

Brown, L.D. (1991) NGOs as bridging organizations: a complex role. *IMPACT* No.14.

Budden, M. (1986) *Tanseed: Report and Recommendations.* Tanzania Seed Company Ltd., Arusha.

Carr, S.J. (1989) Technology for small-scale farmers in sub-Saharan Africa. *Technical Paper* No.109, The World Bank, Washington D.C.

Chambers, R. (1991) Scientist or Resource-Poor Farmer – Whose Knowledge Counts? Paper presented at a seminar on Crop Protection for Resource-Poor Farmers, 4–8 November, Isle of Thorns, UK. CTA/NRI, Wageningen and Kent, UK.

Chibasa, W.M. (1985) Zambia Seed Company: The Maize Seed Situation in Zambia. Paper presented at first Eastern, Central and Southern Africa Regional Maize Workshop, 10–17 March, CIMMYT, Lusaka.

CIAT (1982) *Proceedings of the Conference on Improved Seed for the Small Farmer* 9–13 August, Cali, Colombia. CIAT, Cali, Colombia.

CIAT (1992) Farmer Participatory Research and the Development of an Improved Bean Seed Strategy in Rwanda. Paper prepared for workshop on Farmer Participatory Research, 17–19 February, Addis Ababa, Ethiopia.

CIMMYT (1987) *1986 World Maize Facts and Trends: The Economics of Commercial Maize Seed Production in Developing Countries*. CIMMYT, Mexico D.F.

CIMMYT (1990) *1989 World Maize Facts and Trends: Realizing the Potential of Maize in Sub-Saharan Africa*. CIMMYT, Mexico D.F.

Collinson, M. (1989) Small farmers and technology in Eastern and Southern Africa. *Journal of International Development* 1(1), 66–82.

Commander, S. (ed.) (1989) *Structural Adjustment and Agriculture: Theory and Practice in Africa and Latin America*. ODI with James Currey and Heinemann, London.

Conway, G. and Barbier, E. (1990) *After the Green Revolution: Sustainable Agriculture for Development*. Earthscan, London.

Cooper, D., Vellvé, R. and Hobbelink, H. (1992) *Growing Diversity: Genetic Resources and Local Food Security*. Intermediate Technology Publications, London.

Cromwell, E. (ed.) (1990) Seed diffusion mechanisms in small farmer communities: lessons from Asia, Africa and Latin America. *Network Paper* No.21, Agricultural Administration (Research and Extension) Network, Overseas Development Institute, London.

Cromwell, E. (1992a) The impact of economic reform on the performance of the seed sector in Eastern and Southern Africa. OECD Development Centre *Technical Paper* No.68. OECD Development Centre, Paris.

Cromwell, E. (1992b) Malawi, In: Duncan, A. and Howell, J. (eds) *Structural Adjustment and the African Farmer*. James Currey, London.

Cromwell, E. (1993) The political economy of international agricultural research. *Development Policy Review* 11, 109–114.

Cromwell, E. and Wiggins, S. with Wentzel, S. (1993) *Sowing Beyond the State: NGOs and Seed Supply in Developing Countries*. Overseas Development Institute, London.

DanAgro (1987) Malawi, Southern African Development Coordination Conference Regional Seed Production and Supply Project Vol. IID. DanAgro, Copenhagen.

DanAgro (1990) Southern African Development Coordination Conference (SADCC) Regional Seed Production and Supply Project Vol. 1A. DanAgro, Copenhagen.

Dean, E. (1966) *The Supply Response of African Farmers: Theory and Measurement in Malawi*. North Holland Publishing Company, Amsterdam.

de Boef, W., Amanor, K., Wellard, K., with Bebbington, A. (1994) *Cultivating Knowledge*. Intermediate Technology Publications, London.

Delouche, J.C. (1982) Seed Quality Guidelines for the Small Farmer. Paper presented for the CIAT – Seed Unit Workshop, 9–13 August 1982.

Douglas, J.E. (ed.) (1980) *Successful Seed Programs: a Planning and Management Guide*. Westview Press, Boulder, Colorado.

Dougnac, M. and Kokwe, M. (1988) Traditional Methods used for Seed Collection, Storage, Supply and their Relationships to Current Developments in Seed Supply Systems. Paper presented at seminar on Organization of Seed Production and Supply, 30 January–10 February, Svalof/BITS, Lusaka.

Edwards, R., Gibson, P., Kean, S., Lubasi, C. and Waterworth, J. (1988) Improving small-scale farmers' maize production in Zambia: experiences in collaboration between commodity research, adaptive research and extension workers. *CIMMYT Farming Systems Newsletter* No.32.

ENDA (1990) *Zimbabwe Seed Action Network Annual Report, 1988–89*. ENDA, Harare.

Erikson, J., Mwanza, O., Svensson, O. and Walton, I. (1989) Research and seed programme within ASSP. GRZ/SIDA evaluation mission. *Working Paper* No.14, International Rural Development Centre, Swedish University of Agricultural Sciences, Uppsala.

Eurostat/Federal Statistical Office (1990) *Report Zimbabwe 1990*. Office for Official Publications of the European Communities, Luxembourg.

Evenson, R.E. and David, C. (1993) *Adjustment and Technology: the Case of Rice*. OECD Development Centre, Paris, France.

FAO (1987) *A Manual on Seed Marketing Management in Developing Countries*. Marketing and Credit Service, Agricultural Services Division, FAO, Rome.

FAO (1994) FAO *Seed Review 1989–90*. Food and Agriculture Organization of the United Nations, Rome.

Farmer, B. (ed.) (1977) *Green Revolution?* Macmillan, London.

Farrington, J., Bebbington, A., Lewis, D. and Wellard, K. (1993) *Reluctant Partners? NGOs and the State in Sustainable Agricultural Development*. Routledge, London.

Ferguson, A.E. (1992) Differences among women farmers: implications for African agricultural research programs. *CRSP Working Paper 92/3,* Michigan State University. Bean/Cowpea CRSP, East Lansing, Michigan.

Friis-Hansen, E. (1988) Seeds of wealth, seeds of risk – vulnerability of hybrid maize production in the Southern Highlands of Tanzania. *Project Paper* No 88.3, Centre for Development Research, Copenhagen.

Friis-Hansen, E. (1990) *The Zimbabwe Seed Industry*. Background study for the World Bank agricultural sector review of Zimbabwe (mimeo).

Friis-Hansen, E., Bendsen, E., Sass, H. and Dickens, J. (1991) Four Agricultural Training Institutes, Zimbabwe. *Evaluation Report* No. 1991/3. DANIDA, Copenhagen.

Gebrekidan, B. and Kebede, Y. (1979) The traditional culture and yield potentials of the Ethiopian high lysine sorghums. *Ethiopian Journal of Agricultural Science* 1(1).

Gerhart, J. (1975) *The Diffusion of Hybrid Maize in Western Kenya*. CIMMYT, Mexico.

Gore, C.H. (1987) Summary report of ENDA–Zimbabwe's Indigenous Small Grains Programme. In: AGRITEX/GTZ (eds) *Cropping in Semi-Arid Areas of Zimbabwe*. Proceedings of a workshop held in Harare, 24–28 August 1987 Masvingo. GTZ Agricultural and Rural Development Team, Zimbabwe.

Government of Malawi (1987) *National Physical Development Plan*, Vol. Government Printer, Zomba.

Government of Malawi (1989) *Producer Price Proposals for Smallholder Agricultural Commodities and Inputs for the 1989/90 Growing Season*. Planning Division, Ministry of Agriculture, Lilongwe.

Government of Republic of Zambia (1994) *Economic Report 1993*. National Commission for Development Planning, Lusaka.

Green, T. (1987) Farmer-to-farmer seed exchange in the Eastern Hills of Nepal: the case of 'Pokhreli Masino' rice. *Working Paper* 05/87. Pakhribas Agricultural Centre, Dhankuta, Nepal.

Gregg, B.R., Delouche, J.C. and Bunch, H.D. (1980) Inter-relationships of the essential activities of a stable, efficient seed industry. *Seed Science and Technology* 8, 207–227.

Groosman, A. (ed.) (1988) Seed industry development: developing countries' experiences in different crops. *IVO Research Report* No. 34, Institut voor Ontwikkelingen vraagstukken, Tilburg, Netherlands.

Groosman, A., Linnemann, A. and Wierema, H. (1988) Technology development and changing seed supply systems: seminar proceedings. *Research Report* No.27, IVO, Tilburg, Netherlands.

Gulhati, R. (1991) Impasse in Zambia. *Public Administration and Development* 11(3).

Heisey, P. (ed.) (1990) Accelerating the transfer of wheat breeding gains to farmers: a study of the dynamics of varietal replacement in Pakistan. *CIMMYT Research Report* No.1, CIMMYT, Mexico.

Heisey, P.W. and Brennan, J.P. (1991) An analytical model of farmers demand for replacement seed. *American Journal of Agricultural Economics* 73(4).

Jaffee, J. (1991) *The Balance Between Public and Private Sector Activities in Seed Supply Systems*. The World Bank, Washington D.C. (mimeo).

JSSA (1989) Seed Production for the small-scale farming sector in Africa. *Journal of The Swedish Seed Association* Special Issue, 99(4).

Kaimowitz, D. (ed.) (1990) *Making the Link: Agricultural Research and Technology Transfer in Developing Countries*. Westview/International Service for National Agricultural Research, Boulder, CO.

Kanungwe, M.B. (1989) Seed Production and Distribution in Zambia: Organization, Progress and Problems with Special Reference to Small Scale Family Farming. Paper presented at seminar on Organization of Seed Production and Supply, 30 January–10 February, Svalof/BITS, Lusaka.

Kelly, A.F. (1989) *Seed Planning and Policy for Agricultural Production*. Belhaven Press, UK.

Kydd, J. (1988) Policy reform and adjustment in an economy under siege: Malawi, 1980–87. *IDS Bulletin* 19(1).

Lawrence, P. (1988) The Green Revolution in Africa: stagnation or diffusion? *Background Paper* No.12, African Development Group, School of Oriental and African Studies, University of London.

Lehman, H.P. (1990) The politics of adjustment in Kenya and Zimbabwe: the State as intermediary. *Studies in Comparative International Development* 25(3).

Lipton, M. and Longhurst, R. (1989) *New Seeds and Poor People*. Unwin Hyman, London.

Low, A. (1986) *Agricultural Development in Southern Africa: Farm–Household Economics and the Food Crisis*. James Currey, London.

Low, A. and Waddington, S. (1990) Maize adaptive research: achievements and prospects in Southern Africa. *Farming Systems Bulletin* No.6.

McMullen, N. (1987) *Seeds and World Agricultural Progress*. National Planning Association, Washington, D.C.

McNeely, J.A., Miller, K.R., Reid, W.V. Mittermeir, R.A. and Werner, T.B. (1990) *Conserving the World's Biological Diversity*. The International Union for the

Conservation of Nature and Natural Resources, World Resources Institute, Conservation International, World Wildlife Fund - US and the World Bank, Gland, Switzerland and Washington D.C.

Marter, A. and Honeybone, D. (1976) *The Economic Resources of Rural Households and the Distribution of Agricultural Development (Zambia)*. Rural Development Studies Bureau, University of Zambia, Lusaka.

Mellor, J.W. (1988) *Agricultural Development Opportunities for the 1990s – the Role of Research*. Address presented at International Centers Week of the Consultative Group on International Agricultural Research, Washington D.C., 4 November 1988 (mimeo).

MLARR (1990) *Farm Management Survey of Zimbabwe*. Ministry of Lands, Agriculture and Rural Resettlement, Harare.

Moberg, S. (1994) The research and seed project in Zambia. *IRDC Currents* 7.

Mosley, P., Harrigan, J. and Toye, J. (1991) *Aid and Power: the World Bank and Policy-based Lending*. Routledge, London.

Mpande, R. (1992) Conservation of local seed varieties: a food security strategy for the small-scale farmer in Zimbabwe. In: Proceedings of Conference *The Gene Traders – Security or Profit in Food Production*. SOAS, London, 14–15 April 1992. Intermediate Technology and New Economics Foundation.

Muliokela, S.W. and Kaliangile, I. (n.d.) The Zambia seed industry: issues and opportunities (mimeo).

MSU (1987) *Malawi Collaborative Research Support Project Detailed Annual Report*. Bean/Cowpea CRSP Management Office, Michigan State University, East Lansing.

Mwanaumo, A. (1989) Support by the Government to the Zambian Seed Industry and to the Small Scale Farmer. Paper presented at seminar on Organization of Seed Production and Supply, 30 January–10 February, Svalof/BITS, Lusaka.

National Seed Company of Malawi (1990) *Seeds Catalogue 1990/91*. National Seed Company of Malawi, Lilongwe.

NEF (1988) Douenza Seed Bank Workshop, 19–20 January, Near East Foundation, Douenza, Mali.

Norrby, S. (1986) Appraisal and evaluation of the Swedish support to the Zambian Seed Programme: A cost–benefit analysis. A research paper written in partial fulfilment of the requirements for obtaining the degree of Master of Business Administration from the Research Institute of Management Science, Delft University of Technology, The Netherlands.

Nyongesa, T.E. and Johnson, S. (1990) The Acceptability of New Seed Varieties: Report of a Survey to Determine Farmers' Response to New Seed Varieties. EMI Projects, Embu, Kenya (mimeo).

Osborn, T. (1990) Multi-institutional approaches to participatory technology development: a case study from Senegal. Agricultural Administration (Research and Extension) *Network Paper* No.13, Overseas Development Institute, London.

Paul, S. (1992) Accountability in public services: exit, voice and control. *World Development* 20(7).

Pray, C.E. and Ramaswami, B. (1991) A framework for seed policy analysis in developing countries. *IFPRI Policy Paper*, International Food Policy Research Institute, Washington D.C.

Rees, D.P., Dales, M.J. and Golob, P. (1992) *Alternative Methods for the Control of Stored Product Pests: a Bibliographic Database*. NRI, Chatham, UK.

Republic of The Gambia (1987) Agricultural Inputs Sub-Sector Programme. Paper presented at a Conference of Donors on Agriculture, Banjul, October.

Richards, P. (1985) *Indigenous Agricultural Revolution.* Hutchinson, London.

Ristanovic, D. (1989) Maize Varieties in Zambia and Their Acceptance by Farmers. Paper presented at the First Svalov/BITS Follow-Up Seminar on Organisation and Management of Seed Production and Supply, Lusaka, 30 January–10 February.

Rusike, J. (1995) An institutional analysis of the maize seed industry in Southern Africa. A dissertation submitted to Michigan State University in partial fulfillment of the requirements for the degree of Doctor of Philosophy.

Sandland, O.T. and Schei, P.J. (eds) (1993) *Proceedings of the Norway/UNEP Expert Conference on Biodiversity, Trondheim, Norway,* 24–28 May 1993.

Shapiro, K.H. (1977) Efficiency Differentials in Peasant Agriculture and their Implications for Development Policies. Paper presented at the 16th International Conference of Agricultural Economics, Institute of Agricultural Economics, Oxford.

Sibale, P.K. and Mtambo, P.J. (1989) Production of Certified Chitembana and Mawanga Groundnut Seed by the Smallholder Farmers: Malawi Experience. Paper presented at the third regional workshop of Groundnut Research and Improvement in Southern Africa, CIMMYT, Lusaka.

SIDA (1991) *Review of the Seed Sector.* Swedish International Development Authority, Stockholm.

Simmonds, N.W. (1979) *Principles of Crop Improvement.* Longman, U.K.

Singh, R. (1990) *A Preparatory Note for Rapid Rural Seed Appraisal.* Band Aid/Action Aid/University of Edinburgh Seed Technology Unit SEED Project, Addis Ababa, Ethiopia.

Smale, M. with Kaunda, Z.H.W., Makina, H.L., Mkandawire, M.M.M.K., Msowoya, M.N.S, Mwale, D.J.E.K. and Heisey, P.W. (1991) Chimanga Cha Makolo, hybrids, and composites: an analysis of farmers' adoption of maize technology in Malawi 1989–91. *CIMMYT Economic Working Paper* 91/04. CIMMYT, Mexico D.F.

Smith, A. and Thomson, T. (1991) Achieving a Reasonable Balance Between the Public and Private Sectors in Agriculture. Paper presented at 21st International Conference of Agricultural Economists, Tokyo, Japan, 22–29 August.

Sperling, L. (1993) *Analysis of Bean Seed Channels in the Great Lakes Region: South Kivu, Zaire, Southern Rwanda, and Select Bean-growing Zones of Burundi (summary report).* CIAT Regional Programme, Butare, Rwanda.

Sperling, L., Scheidegger, U., Ntambouura, B., Musungayi, T. and Murhandikire, J.M. (1992) *Analysis of Bean Seed Channels in South Kivu, Zaire and Butare and Gikongoro Prefectures, Rwanda.* CIAT and Programme National Légumineuses, Rwanda.

Swanson, T.M., Pearce, D.W. and Cervigny, R. (1994) *The Valuation and Appropriation of the Global Benefits of Plant Genetic Resources for Agriculture.* A report to the FAO Commission on Plant Genetic Resources by the Centre for Social and Economic Research on the Global Environment, Cambridge.

Timothy, D.H., Harvey, P.H. and Dowswell, C.R. (1988) *Development and Spread of Improved Maize Varieties and Hybrids in Developing Countries.* Agency for International Development, Washington D.C.

Tripp, R. (1995) Seed regulatory frameworks and resource-poor farmers: a literature review. *Network Paper* No. 51, Agricultural Administration (Research and Extension) Network, Overseas Development Institute, London.

USC (1988) *African Seeds of Survival Programme: Project Proposal.* Unitarian Service Committee, Ottawa.

van Oosterhout, S. (1992) How the Hegemony of Western Science Has Limited the

Development of Dynamic Conservation of Indigenous Sorghum Landraces. Paper presented at CTA/IBPGR/KARI/UNEP Seminar on *Safeguarding the Genetic Basis of Africa's Traditional Crops*, Nairobi, 5–9 October.

van Oosterhout, S. (1996) What does in-situ conservation mean in the life of a small-scale farmer? Paper presented at a workshop on 'Using Diversity' held in New Delhi, India, 19–21 June 1995. IDRC.

Variety Release Committee (1986) *A Description of Crop Varieties Grown in Malawi*. Variety Release Committee, Department of Agricultural Research, Ministry of Agriculture, Lilongwe.

Walker, J.T. (1980) Philosophies affecting the spread and development of seed production. In: Hebblethwaite, P.D. (ed.) *Seed Production*. Proceedings of Twenty-Eighth Easter School in Agricultural Science, Nottingham, UK.

Wiggins, S. and Cromwell, E. (1995) Non-Governmental Organizations and seed provision to smallholders in developing countries. *World Development* 23(3).

World Bank (1986) Malawi: Improving Agricultural Marketing and Food Security Policies – A Reform Proposal. *Report No. 6083-MAI*, World Bank, Washington D.C.

World Bank (1987) Project performance audit report: Pakistan: Seed project (Credit 620–PAK), *Report No.6780*, Operations Evaluation Department, The World Bank, Washington D.C.

World Bank (1989) Malawi: National Rural Development Programme (NRDP) Technical Issues Review *Report No.7539-MAI*, World Bank, Washington D.C.

World Bank (1990) *World Tables 1989–90 Edition*. World Bank, Washington D.C.

Wright, M., Donaldson, T., Cromwell, E. and New, J. (1994) *The Retention and Care of Seeds by Small-scale Farmers*. NRI, Chatham, UK.

Young, R. and Loxley, J. (1990) *Zambia: An Assessment of Zambia's Structural Adjustment Experience*. The North–South Institute, Ottawa.

Personal communications

Dr Stephen Muliokela and Mr Simon Mwale, Seed Control & Certification Institute, Chilanga, Zambia.

Mr Simon Croxton, Intermediate Technology and Development Group, Rugby, UK.

Mr Peter Tyler, Natural Resources Institute, Chatham, UK.

Ms Melinda Smale, CIMMYT, Lilongwe, Malawi.

Ms Christian Renton, ACORD, Sudan.

Dr. Batson Zambezi, Chitedze Research Station, Lilongwe, Malawi.

Appendix 1
Technical Features of Seed Production

1.1 The Nature of Improvement in MV Seed

There are two sources of potential improvement in seeds, which together make up the 'quality' of seed:

1. the **genetic information** contained within the seed itself;
2. the **physical and physiological** attributes of the seed lot – purity, germination capacity, vigour, health and freedom from disease.

These are independent of each other but both are required for MV seed to contribute fully to better crop production performance. Thus genetic quality is the ultimate determinant of performance but, if physical quality is poor, the benefit of improved genetic potential cannot be realised. The relative importance of genetic and physical quality varies: in one farming system, the most important need may be for seed with assured genetic potential; in another, the genetic quality of an established variety may be quite adequate but storage difficulties or pest and disease problems may still enable the formal seed sector to supply a useful product, by concentrating on physiological quality. However, poor management of multiplication and processing can reduce the extent formal sector seed is an improvement on what farmers can save on-farm themselves.

The concept of 'variety' (a theoretically infinite population of individuals sharing a defined set of characteristics) is fundamental to formal sector seed production and is one of the major factors distinguishing it from informal seed supply systems, which use less precise material of local origin. The availability of genetically superior varieties from the research system is a major impetus to the establishment and sustainability of the formal seed sector. At the same time, an over-emphasis on genetic progress can create tensions within seed organisations. From the marketing perspective, it is profitable to trade on novelty by constantly providing new varieties, even if the real advantage to farmers is small (the example of rice in South East Asia is frequently quoted in this context). However, for ease of production, a few really successful varieties – here *SR52* hybrid maize in Zimbabwe is often cited – are preferable.

1.2 Seed Production for Different Crop Species

The two fundamental characteristics of crop species that determine the scale and complexity of seed production are the breeding system of the crop and its multiplication factor. These and other important biological features of the major food crops grown in small farm farming systems are summarised in Appendix Table 1.1.

1.2.1 Multiplication factor

This is the net increase in the quantity of seed achieved in one generation and it determines the number of generations required to produce seed in usable quantities. Breeding institutions are not in a position to produce enough seed to satisfy total national requirements and, typically, three to five generations of multiplication are needed to achieve this.

Crops such as maize, sorghum and millet, which have a high multiplication factor (normally correlated with small seed size and low sowing rate per hectare), are easier for the formal seed sector to deal with because fewer multiplications are required and, at each stage, there are smaller quantities to process, store and distribute. Because of the low sowing rates, the purchase cost to farmers as a proportion of total production costs per hectare is normally lower and therefore it is feasible to charge a higher price for such seed.

Grain legumes are characterised by low multiplication factors, because of their large seeds and low yields, and these are consequently the least attractive crops for commercial seed companies to handle. The extreme example is groundnuts, with a multiplication factor of less than 10 and a bulky seed which is prone to mechanical damage. Furthermore, the technical justification for formal sector groundnut seed production is weak since the crop is strongly self-pollinated (see below) so farmers can maintain seed successfully on-farm themselves.

1.2.2 Breeding system

This determines the ease of maintaining the genetic integrity of a variety and consequently it affects seed quality as opposed to the quantitative aspects of seed production. The majority of cereal crops, including rice, wheat and barley, are normally self-pollinated, as are virtually all legumes. The exceptions which are cross-pollinated include maize, sorghum, millet and sunflower and, in the legumes, pigeon peas.

Generally, self-pollinated crops are easy to handle because they naturally exist as pure lines and are genetically homozygous. If variability does occur from any

Appendix Table 1.1: Important biological features of major crop species

	Hybrid Maize	Open Pollinated Maize	Sorghum/Millet	Wheat	Rice	Beans	Groundnuts
Breeding system	Controlled pollination	Cross-pollination	Intermediate	Self-pollination	Self-pollination	Self-pollination	Self-pollination
Sowing rate per ha	Medium (20kg)	Medium (20kg)	Low (10kg)	High (100kg)	High (50kg)	High (100kg)	High (125kg)
Multiplication factor	High (100)	High (100)	High (100)	Low (25)	Medium (50)	Medium (50)	Very low (<10)
Rate of deterioration	Very rapid	Rapid	Medium	Slow	Slow	Very slow	Very slow
Frequency of purchase	Annual	2 years	3 years	4 years	4 years	Variable	Variable
Availability of improved varieties	Many	Many	Few	Many	Many	Few	Few
Justification for purchase	**Essential**	**Good**	**Variable**	**Poor**	**Poor**	**Poor**	**Very poor**

source (such as from occasional cross-pollinations, mutation or mechanical contamination), it is usually visible and can therefore be eliminated in the process of 'roguing' which is a routine activity in organised seed multiplication. Self-pollinated crops require isolation only to the extent of a physical barrier sufficient to avoid confusion with adjacent crops at sowing and harvest time. It is therefore quite possible to maintain self-pollinating varieties in excellent condition for many years. In the mid-1970s, for example, samples of the barley variety *Proctor* in Kenya and Ethiopia were found to be perfectly maintained some 20 years after their original release from the UK. Even when varieties have become seriously mixed as a result of uncontrolled multiplication, they can be quickly purified provided that a detailed varietal description exists.

Because of their natural mechanisms of self-pollination, it is complicated and expensive to manipulate these crops on a field scale to produce hybrids, although hybridisation is routinely carried out as part of plant breeding. The notable exception to this is rice, for which hybrid varieties have been available in China for over 20 years – but this technology has not spread to other rice-producing areas. For wheat, barley and virtually all legumes, there are no hybrid crops and no prospect of them in the foreseeable future.

Cross-pollinated crops are more difficult to manage within the formal seed sector because they are intrinsically variable, as a result of their genetic composition, and they are prone to contamination by foreign pollen. To minimise this risk, seed crops have to be isolated from others of the same species. If contamination does occur, it is less easily detected due to the variability which already exists within the variety. The traditional varieties of crops of this kind are 'open-pollinated populations', within which variability is restricted to certain limits to enable the variety to be identified. Such populations can be very difficult to manage because they tend to become more variable in successive multiplications. This variability also makes roguing a difficult task in crops such as maize which, because of its size, is less easily scanned in the field than, say, rice or wheat.

The response to this problem has been to attempt to restrict variability within narrower limits, by means of synthetic or composite varieties, but these still present management problems because of the sustained technical input required to maintain and multiply them. Commercial seed companies are reluctant to undertake this work when equal effort can produce a hybrid which has the benefit of extra vigour and can be sold at a much higher price. There are few examples of well-managed composite varieties – although the maize variety *Katumani* is a composite and this has been maintained satisfactorily in Kenya. However, there are several other old composite varieties still in use in Africa which are now of very uncertain genetic status.

The ultimate solution to the problem of genetic variability is to produce hybrid varieties by controlled crossing of parent lines. This is a labour- and management-intensive activity but does have the advantage of being definable, compared with the techniques required for open-pollinated varieties. Definability is a factor of considerable importance because the formal seed sector cannot deal easily with the intrinsic genetic disorganisation of open-pollinated varieties. Furthermore, hybrid technology has both agronomic (higher yield) and commercial (annual

Appendix Box 1.1: The African seed sector: the special case of hybrid maize seed

We have seen in this Appendix how, because maize is a cross-pollinated crop, MVs for it can only be produced easily by controlling the way that the crop breeds. This control can be achieved in a number of different ways, which are usually named as follows:

Composites: an open-pollinated variety selected from the random combination of a large number of recognised breeding lines or accessions. It has a short breeding cycle, the parental lines do not need to be maintained, and farmers can recycle the seed up to five times before buying fresh seed, *but* it has only intermediate yield potential.

Synthetics: an open-pollinated variety derived from the combination of a number of selected self-pollinated lines. It has at least a 10 year breeding cycle, all parental lines need to be maintained, and farmers can recycle up to three times before buying fresh seed. The yield potential is the same as for composite varieties.

Hybrids: a single, double, or three-way cross of selected inbred lines. Thus, hybrids have similar source material to synthetics and a similar breeding cycle, but fewer parental lines need to be maintained – so less area on the seed farm is needed to maintain the lines. Hybrids have higher yield potential compared with synthetics and composites, but farmers cannot recycle the seed.

'Single', 'double' and 'three-way' cross refer to the number of parents a hybrid has: two parental lines for a single cross; two single crosses for a double cross; and a pure inbred male parent and single cross female parent for a three-way cross. Seed yield is highest from double crosses, intermediate for three-way crosses, and lowest for single crosses.

Non-conventional hybrids: at least one parent is not an inbred line (i.e. one or both are a variety). Top crosses and varietal hybrids are two of the best known non-conventional hybrids. They have a shorter breeding cycle than conventional hybrids and seed production is easier to manage.

Sources: Appendix A in Timothy *et al.*, 1988; Zambezi pers. comm.; CIMMYT, 1987.

---

replacement) advantages and therefore, since the technical opportunities to produce hybrids by controlled pollination exist in precisely those crops which are more difficult to handle conventionally, these technologies have spread rapidly to all candidate species. Appendix Box 1.1 explains the nomenclature used to describe the different ways in which breeding is controlled for maize, the cross-pollinated crop of the greatest importance in the African context.

Appendix Table 1.2: Major nomenclatures for seed generation control

Generation	OECD	AOSCA	Responsibility
1	Breeder	Breeder	Breeder responsible for producing breeder seed from original parental or nucleus material and for maintaining this latter to provide fresh releases
2	Pre-basic	(No direct equivalent)	In the US system, the second generation may be a later multiple of breeder or an earlier multiplication of foundation seed
3	Basic	Foundation	Selected growers produce this generation from supplies provided by the breeder and under their close supervision
4	Certified 1	Registered	Produced on large-scale by seed organisations and sold for commercial crop production. Number of generations of multiplication depends on multiplication factor of particular species but should not be more than 2
5	Certified 2	Certified	Further multiplications outside this controlled generation system, or multiplications that failed to meet quality control standards, are not certified. To maintain this system of multiplication requires a regular release of breeder seed

Note:	OECD	=	Organization for Economic Co-operation and Development
	AOSCA	=	Association of Official Seed Certifying Agencies of the USA

1.3 Generation Control

At a practical level a system for identifying the generations of seed multiplication between breeders and farmers is needed. The control of this multiplication process through a limited number of named generations is a vital aspect of quality control within organised seed production, since it means that the origin of a given crop is always known and faults can be traced. Seed certification provides a comprehensive quality control procedure, involving both field inspection of seed crops and the laboratory testing of seed samples, and is the conventional means for doing this. This requires a standard nomenclature; the two internationally recognised systems are outlined in Appendix Table 1.2.

There are two underlying principles involved in generation control:

1. the number of generations is limited to the minimum necessary to produce

Appendix Table 1.3: Minimum grain : seed price ratios for different crops

Crop		Ratio
Maize:	single cross hybrid	1 : 5
	three-way cross hybrid	1 : 3
	double cross hybrid	1 : 2
Groundnuts		1 : 2
Wheat		1 : 2
Rice		1 : 2

Note:	Factory gate cost (i.e. processed and packed)
	Ratios in Europe and North America are often higher

sufficient seed for farmers without placing undue demands on breeders;
2. 'recycling' of seed at the same generation level is prohibited – it must always proceed down the generation sequence.

Thus, if a variety deteriorates through contamination during multiplication, the damage caused is limited and soon passes out of the system, as fresh stocks of breeder seed are released each year.

Generation control makes effective linkages between the seed producing organisations and the seed certification agencies critically important. It also requires that seed organisations have the capacity to estimate demand for certified seed at least two years in advance, in order to plan breeder and basic seed production accurately.

1.4 Technical and Economic Interactions

Biological factors have a key influence on the costs and benefits associated with seed production. Seed costs are often considered in the form of grain : seed price ratios. Using this approach, in very general terms it is possible to rank the comparative cost of producing different species and varieties of seed, as shown in Appendix Table 1.3.

Thus, the relative attractiveness of seed production to different types of organisation is crop-specific. It also depends on the nature of the cropping pattern in a particular location. MV seed of species with high multiplication factors and low sowing rates, such as maize, sorghum and millet, is cheaper to produce and cheaper for farmers to use. These open-pollinated species also have greater recurrent sales potential than self-pollinated species such as rice, beans and groundnuts. But their production is more difficult to control, so commercial seed companies will tend to promote the use of hybrid varieties of these species, which are more costly and may therefore limit CDR farmers' opportunity for using MV seed.

Where the major crops in the farming system are self-pollinated, recurrent sales of MV seed often depend on the ability of the formal seed sector to provide a steady flow of new varieties to maintain farmer interest. In this case, for the purposes of national development, it may be more effective to devote resources instead to strengthening on-farm seed production and storage facilities.

Environmental conditions also determine the cost of seed processing and storage and they determine whether farmers' main need is for genetic or for physiological improvement in seed quality. In hot, humid conditions, and where a long gap between harvest and planting season makes on-farm seed storage problematic, the more sophisticated processing and storage technology available to the formal seed sector may give it a clear advantage. On the other hand, for regions where the dominant crops can be stored successfully on-farm, the benefit from purchasing seed that has usually been stored for long periods and transported over considerable distances, adding significantly to costs, may be small. The example of rice in lowland tropical environments, especially where double cropping is practised, illustrates this very well.

In Africa, the nature of the interaction between technical and economic factors in the production and supply of seed of hybrid varieties of maize makes the market for hybrid maize seed a special case, compared with the seed market for the other major food crops propagated by true seed.

The visible evidence of this is that, in contrast to other food crops, hybrid maize dominates the land in CDR areas planted to maize over much of Africa. To take two of our case study countries, in Zambia and Zimbabwe our field work suggests that the quantity of hybrid maize seed sold to CDR farmers each year is sufficient to cover all of the maize area in CDR areas, whereas for other crops the quantity of MV seed sold to CDR farmers is sufficient for a relatively small proportion of the plantings in CDR areas (see Tables 6.2 and 7.2).

This is because maize is the only major African food crop propagated by true seed for which technical and economic factors combine in such a way as to make the interests of the formal seed sector and those of farmers in CDR areas coincide. In other words, to use the terminology of Section 3.3 in Chapter 3, it is the only major African food crop propagated by true seed for which there is no market failure in the market for formal sector seed in CDR areas.

There are a number of reasons for this. On the demand side, farmers in CDR areas find purchasing seed of hybrid varieties for their maize crop is attractive for three reasons:

• Hybrid varieties lock in performance, having the potential to increase yields by up to 25% independent of other inputs.
• This increased yield is valuable to CDR farmers because, as national economies depend on maize, MV maize seed and fertiliser tends to be subsidised.
• The low sowing rate of maize means that only small quantities of seed need to be purchased in order to plant a given unit area.

On the supply side, the formal sector finds offering seed of hybrid varieties of maize is profitable for two reasons:

- Maize has a high multiplication factor, so the output of seed per unit area on the seed farm is high and this increases returns to seed production, compared with returns to producing seed for other crops.
- Demand for seed of hybrid varieties of maize is strong, because hybridisation locks in performance, and consistent, because hybrid varieties have a high rate of deterioration and so farmers have to buy fresh seed every year.

As we explained in Section 3.2 of Chapter 3, on neither the demand nor the supply side do these factors hold true for other African food crops.

There are two important implications of this 'special case' situation for the market for seed of hybrid varieties of maize. First, farmers' decision-making processes concerning whether or not to purchase hybrid maize seed are not the same as for other crops: for hybrid maize, there is no choice concerning whether or not to use MV seed – if the decision is made to grow the crop, then seed has to be purchased. Also, in most cases, there has been little choice of supplier until recently – seed of hybrid varieties of maize has been available only from the formal seed sector. Therefore, to use Paul's (1992) criteria for assessing the responsiveness of public services, farmers had little 'voice', or ability to demand change, and no option to 'exit' from the service and find an alternative supplier, in the case of poor performance: as long as subsidisation has kept growing hybrid maize profitable, then farmers have put up with poor seed sector performance.

Second, it is not the case that uptake of MV seed for other crops can or should follow the uptake pattern for hybrid maize seed, either in terms of quantities used or in terms of structure of the seed production and distribution system.

In conclusion, this Appendix has shown that technical and economic factors combine to mean that, with the partial exception of hybrid maize, there is an obvious trade-off between the type of seed that can be produced and sold easily and profitably by the formal sector and that which CDR farmers need. It has also shown that there are important technical reasons why effective linkages between seed organisations and the other institutions with a role in making MV seed available are critically important.

Appendix 2

Example Seed Project Cost-Benefit Analysis

This Appendix demonstrates and explains how a full-scale cost-benefit analysis can be carried out for a regional or national seed project or programme, to support the type of performance assessment outlined in Chapter 4. The illustrative data used are adapted from a real regional seed project. In this case, estimated real financial costs have been used because local factor and product market prices were considered to be relatively undistorted and because the primary concern was with the project's local impact. Where the main aim is to assess the national impact of a project or programme, and/or where market distortions are significant, it would be more appropriate to estimate shadow prices in order to determine economic costs.

The starting point is a computation of the net costs and benefits at household level for farmer users of MV seed, and for contract seed growers if these are used. Examples are given in Appendix Tables 2.2 and 2.3.

For this exercise to be useful, great care must be taken to incorporate values for the non-financial factors outlined in Chapter 4. For example, greater risk of crop failure in poor seasons when using MV seed can be represented as a yield deflator; the less preferred taste of some modern varieties can be represented as a price deflator, etc.

Various other factors must be taken into consideration. Incremental yield estimates are critical and as much care as possible must be taken to ensure that the yield values used are those attainable on CDR farmers' fields (which may not be the same as those obtained by agricultural research departments' on-farm trials).

Grain price differentials may favour or disfavour MV seed depending on local taste preferences. The price of MV seed will always be higher than the cost of local grain used as seed (this latter being the consumer grain price), except where subsidies within the seed production chain keep MV seed prices artificially low. The precise increment will vary between crops and according to government and seed company pricing policies.

Care must be taken to ensure that the sowing and fertiliser application rates used mirror local practice, as this can vary considerably between locations. For the contract growers in the project illustrated here, for example, the incremental cost of growing a seed crop is slightly reduced because of the traditional local practice of

Appendix Table 2.1: Example calculation of MV seed area coverage

	Year 1	Year 2	Year 3	Year 4
Seed produced (tonnes)	10	15	20	25
Sowing rate (kg/ha)	50	50	50	50
Area coverage (ha)	200	300	400	500
Adjusted for replacement rate (4 years) (ha)	200	500	900	1,100

sowing grain crops at higher plant populations for subsequent thinning as green fodder.

For simplicity, the examples given here assume that in one year only one pure stand crop of rice, maize, wheat or potatoes is grown on each parcel of land. This is not realistic for many farming systems in CDR areas, where multiple inter-planted crops are the norm. More accurate figures would be obtained by valuing total annual production costs and benefits from one hectare under the main cropping patterns; in this example, 'maize' could be replaced by 'maize/millet-fallow'.

The net incremental costs and net incremental benefits obtained from these calculations are then fed into the main cost-benefit analysis given in Appendix Table 2.4. However, as well as doing this, it is critically important to assess how CDR farmers are likely to react to these apparent costs and benefits of using MV seed. There are two main determinants of this: farmers' reaction to the perceived risk associated with the change; and their reaction to the relative rate of return to different factors of production – both of which have been the subject of considerable theoretical and empirical debate.

Some of the most commonly used comparative indicators are illustrated in Appendix Table 2.2. The marginal cost-benefit ratio (MCBR) and the marginal rate of return (MRR) relate primarily to risk assessment. The MCBR shows the difference between the gross benefits and variable costs of using MV seed compared with using saved seed. In the example given here, changing to using modern variety maize seed is clearly not worthwhile.

The MRR shows the percentage difference between the net benefits and variable costs. Ashworth (1990) suggests that in Zimbabwe a minimum MRR of 60% is needed, even in relatively high potential areas, for CDR farmers to buy MV seed and secure an income equivalent to the minimum daily wage.

For CDR farmers who have few resources under their control other than domestic labour and who are severely cash-constrained, neither of these aggregate indicators may be as relevant as the relative return to individual factors of production. This is clearly illustrated in Appendix Table 2.2, where returns to cash invested (in supplies of purchased MV seed and fertiliser) are high but returns to labour – which is the

Appendix Table 2.2: Partial budgets for seed users by crop (Shs/ha)

	Rice		Maize		Wheat		Potatoes	
	FV seed	MV seed	FV seed	MV seed	FV seed	MV seed	FV seed	MV seed
Yield (kg/ha)	2,500.00	3,000.00	1,300.00	1,700.00	1,100.00	2,200.00	4,000.00	8,000.00
Less milling adj. (%)	40.00	40.00	10.00	10.00	10.00	10.00	0.00	0.00
Price (Shs/kg)	14.00	17.00	8.00	6.00	7.00	7.00	6.00	6.00
Total benefit	21,000.00	30,600.00	9,360.00	9,180.00	6,930.00	13,860.00	24,000.00	48,000.00
Seed amount (kg/ha)	60.00	60.00	30.00	30.00	120.00	120.00	900.00	900.00
Seed price (Shs/kg)	14.00	20.00	8.00	10.00	7.00	9.00	6.00	12.00
Seed cost (Shs/ha)	840.00	1,200.00	240.00	300.00	840.00	1,080.00	5,400.00	10,800.00
Fertiliser (kg/ha)	0.00	60.00	0.00	50.00	50.00	50.00	0.00	0.00
Fertiliser price (Shs/kg)	5.85	5.85	5.85	5.85	5.85	5.85	5.85	5.85
Fertiliser cost (Shs/ha)	0.00	351.00	0.00	292.50	292.50	292.50	0.00	0.00
Labour (days/ha)	81.00	108.00	122.00	162.00	95.00	126.00	169.00	225.00
Labour cost (Shs/day)	25.00	25.00	25.00	25.00	25.00	25.00	25.00	25.00
Labour cost (Shs/ha)	2,025.00	2,700.00	3,050.00	4,050.00	2,375.00	3,150.00	4,225.00	5,625.00

resource households generally have better access to – are much less and in all cases lower than the average daily off-farm wage rate of Shs25.

This type of distributional issue is critically important in interpreting the overall results of the cost-benefit analysis. Turning to Appendix Table 2.4, we can construct this overall analysis using the seed users' and contract growers' data.

Start by calculating the total area of each crop that can be planted using the MV seed produced by the project. This requires annual project seed production per crop to be divided by the sowing rate for each crop and the result to be added cumulatively, allowing for the typical seed replacement rate used by farmers within the project area. For rice, for example, this might be as shown in Appendix Table 2.1.

The net incremental costs and benefits of using MV seed on this area can be taken from Appendix Table 2.2, to value production benefits and on-farm variable production costs, as shown in Appendix Table 2.4. Ideally, these costs and benefits should be valued only for that part of the project's seed production which is known to have been used as seed, i.e. allowing for any spoilage in store, sales as food grain, etc.; in most cases, this will be difficult to assess and it will be necessary to approximate by valuing total MV seed production instead.

Where improving CDR farmers' incomes by involving them in MV seed production as contract growers has been an important project objective, it will be necessary in addition to measure the total area used for MV seed production in order to make a similar valuation of the net incremental costs and benefits of MV seed production, using the data from Appendix Table 2.3.

To these calculations, the costs of the project itself must be added. These are indicated in Appendix Table 2.4 under capital costs and project recurrent costs (salaries, etc.). Whilst these costs will occur only during the project life (Years 1–4 in the example given in Appendix Table 2.4), it is important to allow for the continuing occurrence of on-farm costs and benefits for the full life of the MV seed produced; this will vary between crops, depending on the seed replacement rate used by farmers in the project area.

Having estimated all the relevant costs and benefits, the project or programme can be subjected to the usual performance assessment, using the appropriate indicators. The example given here shows an internal rate of return of over 100% which, in terms of conventional project analysis, is of course remarkably high. This illustrates two limitations to the use of conventional cost-benefit analysis for MV seed projects and programmes. Firstly, where data are poor, so computations have been based on best estimates, it will be important to carry out a thorough sensitivity analysis (not shown here); in the case of formal sector seed projects and programmes, the key variables to work on are yields, MV seed prices and grain prices. Secondly, even where data are known to be accurate, the long-term benefits of producing and distributing MV seed that is genuinely relevant to local CDR farmers' needs – as with agricultural research projects and programmes with the same ultimate aim – obviously outweigh the limited project investment costs required.

Appendix Table 2.3: Partial budgets for seed producers by crop (Shs/ha)

Crop	Rice		Maize	
	Grain	*Seed*	*Grain*	*Seed*
Seed yield (kg/ha)	0.00	1,000.00	0.00	665.00
Price (Shs/kg)	0.00	20.00	0.00	10.00
Grain yield (kg/ha)	1,800.00	1,200.00	1,530.00	931.50
Price (Shs/kg)	17.00	17.00	6.00	6.00
Total benefit	30,600.00	40,400.00	9,180.00	12,239.00
Production costs	60.00	50.00	30.00	30.00
Source seed (kg/ha)	17.00	20.00	6.00	10.00
Price (Shs/kg)	1,020.00	1,000.00	180.00	300.00
Seed cost (Shs/ha)	60.00	60.00	50.00	90.00
Fertiliser (kg/ha)	5.85	5.85	5.85	5.85
Fert. price (Shs/kg)	351.00	351.00	292.50	526.50
Fert. cost (Shs/ha)	0.00	10.00	0.00	2.00
Crop prot. (kg/ha)	0.00	13.00	0.00	150.00
Price (Shs/kg)	0.00	130.00	0.00	300.00
Cost (Shs/ha)	108.00	120.00	162.00	180.00
Labour (days/ha)	25.00	25.00	25.00	25.00
Cost (Shs/day)	2,700.00	3,000.00	4,050.00	4,500.00
Cost (Shs/ha)				
Proc.mkting costs	0.00	60.00	0.00	72.00
Extra transp./ha	0.00	0.25	0.00	0.25
Extra transp. cost/kg	0.00	15.00	0.00	18.00
Extra transp. cost/ha	0.00	2.00	0.00	2.00
Store chems./ha	0.00	1.50	0.00	1.50
Store chems.cost	0.00	3.00	0.00	3.00
Cost/ha				
Total variable cost	4,071.00	4,499.00	4,522.50	5,647.50
Net benefit	26,529.00	35,901.00	4,657.50	6,591.50

Appendix Table 2.3 cont.: Partial budgets for seed producers by crop (Shs/ha)

	Wheat		Potatoes	
Crop	Grain	Seed	Grain	Seed
Seed yield (kg/ha)	0.00	800.00	0.00	2,800.00
Price (Shs/kg)	0.00	9.00	0.00	12.00
Grain yield (kg/ha)	1,980.00	1,260.00	8,000.00	5,200.00
Price (Shs/kg)	7.00	7.00	6.00	5.76
Total benefit	13,860.00	16,020.00	48,000.00	63,552.00
Production costs	120.00	100.00	900.00	1,800.00
Source seed (kg/ha)	7.00	9.00	6.00	12.00
Price (Shs/kg)	840.00	900.00	5,400.00	21,600.00
Seed cost (Shs/ha)	50.00	90.00	0.00	250.00
Fertiliser (kg/ha)	5.85	5.85	0.00	5.85
Fert. price (Shs/kg)	292.50	526.50	0.00	1,462.50
Fert. cost (Shs/ha)	0.00	0.00	0.00	2.00
Crop prot. (kg/ha)	0.00	0.00	0.00	25.00
Price (Shs/kg)	0.00	0.00	0.00	50.00
Cost (Shs/ha)	126.00	140.00	225.00	250.00
Labour (days/ha)	25.00	25.00	25.00	25.00
Cost (Shs/day)	3,150.00	3,500.00	5,625.00	6,250.00
Cost (Shs/ha)				
Proc.mkting costs	0.00	140.00	0.00	2,052.00
Extra transp./ha	0.00	0.25	0.00	0.25
Extra transp. cost/kg	0.00	35.00	0.00	513.00
Extra transp. cost/ha				
Store chems./ha	0.00	2.00	0.00	0.00
Store chems.cost	0.00	1.50	0.00	0.00
Cost/ha	0.00	3.00	0.00	0.00
Total variable cost	4,282.50	4,964.50	11,025.00	29,875.50
Net benefit	9,577.50	11,055.50	36,975.00	33,676.50

Appendix Table 2.4: Seeds programme costs and benefits (Shs'000 real prices)

Item	Year 1	Year 2	Year 3	Year 4
Benefits				
Rice	283	852	2,281	5,843
Maize	357	1,229	3,115	9,334
Wheat	0	1,707	3,167	5,188
Potatoes	0	0	0	635
Total	640	3,788	8,563	21,000
Costs				
Capital costs				
Buildings	600	0	0	0
Equipment	400	100	100	0
Total	1,000	100	100	0
Recurrent costs				
On-farm costs				
Rice	30	92	246	631
Maize	261	897	2,274	6,812
Wheat	0	822	1,526	2,500
Potatoes	0	0	0	254
Total	291	1,811	4,046	10,197
Salaries & allows.	800	850	900	950
Supplies & fuel	400	450	500	550
Rent & repairs	100	110	120	130
Contingencies	13	14	14	14
Total	1,313	1,424	1,534	1,644
Total costs	2,604	3,335	5,680	11,841
Net cash flow	-1,964	453	2,883	9,159
NPV at 15%	15,771			
IRR/100	1.34			

Appendix Table 2.4 cont.: Seeds programme costs and benefits (Shs'000 real prices)

Item	Year 5	Year 6	Total
Benefits			
Rice	5,984	5,780	
Maize	9,706	9,425	
Wheat	5,706	3,757	
Potatoes	699	762	
Total	22,095	19,724	75,810
Costs			
Capital costs			
Buildings	0	0	
Equipment	0	0	
Total	0	0	1,200
Recurrent costs			
On-farm costs			
Rice	647	625	
Maize	7,084	6,878	
Wheat	2,749	1,810	
Potatoes	279	305	
Total	10,759	9,618	36,722
Salaries & allows.	0	0	
Supplies & fuel	0	0	
Rent & repairs	0	0	
Contingencies	0	0	
Total	0	0	5,915
Total costs	10,759	9,618	43,837
Net cash flow	11,336	10,106	31,973
NPV at 15%	15,771		
IRR/100	1.34		

Appendix 3

Seed Sector Statistics for Malawi, Zambia and Zimbabwe

Appendix Table 3.1: Maize prices in Malawi, Zambia and Zimbabwe (US$/kg 1984/85 – 1988/89)

Constant prices		1984/85	1985/86	1986/87	1987/88
Producer price for grain					
Malawi		0.09	0.06	0.05	0.06
Zambia			0.09	0.05	0.04
Zimbabwe		0.15	0.13	0.12	0.11
Seed price					
Malawi	Three way cross				0.30
	Single cross	0.71	0.52	0.45	0.35
Zambia	Three way cross				0.18
	Single cross				0.35
Zimbabwe	Three way cross	0.46	0.45	0.41	0.36
	Single cross	0.93	0.90	0.83	0.72
Fertiliser price					
Malawi		0.22	0.20	0.17	0.17
Zambia				0.04	
Zimbabwe		0.26	0.25	0.23	0.20

Source: Ministry of Agriculture and seed company records in Malawi, Zambia and Zimbabwe.

Notes: (1) fertiliser = ammonium nitrate (28% nitrogen) for Malawi and Zimbabwe and urea converted to comparable units of nitrogen for Zambia.

(2) blank = no record.

Appendix Table 3.1 cont.: Maize prices in Malawi, Zambia and Zimbabwe
(US$/kg 1984/85 – 1988/89)

Constant prices		1988/89	1989/90	1990/91
Producer price for grain				
Malawi		0.06	0.05	0.05
Zambia		0.05	0.06	0.03
Zimbabwe		0.11	0.07	0.07
Seed price				
Malawi	Three way cross	0.24	0.29	0.35
	Single cross	0.28	0.32	0.39
Zambia	Three way cross	0.32	0.22	0.12
	Single cross	0.57	0.47	0.29
Zimbabwe	Three way cross	0.28	0.30	0.29
	Single cross	0.78	0.61	0.59
Fertiliser price				
Malawi		0.07	0.14	0.16
Zambia			0.13	0.05
Zimbabwe		0.17	0.14	0.15

Source: Ministry of Agriculture and seed company records in Malawi, Zambia and
Zimbabwe.
Notes: (1) fertiliser = ammonium nitrate (28% nitrogen) for Malawi and
Zimbabwe and urea converted to comparable units of nitrogen for
Zambia.
(2) blank = no record.

Appendix Table 3.2: MV seed cost build-up in Malawi, Zambia and Zimbabwe (US$/kg at 1990/91 prices)

	MALAWI		ZAMBIA	ZIMBABWE	
	Single X Hybrid	3 Way Cross Hybrid	All Maize Seed	Single X Hybrid	3 Way Cross Hybrid
Growers' cost	0.37	0.25	n/a	0.47	0.16
Price paid to growers	0.86	0.50	0.35	0.76	0.38
(Growers' margin (%))	(130.00)	(97.00)	n/a	(63.30)	(142.40)
Factory costs	0.35	0.21	0.15	0.11	0.06
Total seed company costs	1.21	0.71	0.50	0.88	0.44
Price paid to seed company	1.07	0.93	0.53	0.65	0.32
(Company margin (%))	(-11.57)	(30.98)	(6.00)	(-26.14)	(-26.10)
Distributors' selling price	0.71	0.65	0.60	0.85	0.42
(Distributors' margin (%))	(-33.60)	(-30.11)	(13.20)	(30.77)	(30.90)

Notes: (1)   Malawi factory costs include cost of field inspections paid for by NSCM.
       (2)   Zimbabwe distributor margin is shown as proportion of discounted price paid for wholesale purchases of small packs (this is lower than Seed Co-op's retail seed price and its prices for larger packs).
       (3)   n/a = not available.

Sources: Ministry of Agriculture and seed company records in Malawi, Zambia and Zimbabwe.

Appendix 4

Assumptions Used in Calculating Economics of Malawi Smallholder Seed Multiplication Scheme

(In 1989/90 MK1 = US$0.36)

1. Inputs: costed at ADMARC input selling prices, including for seed.
2. Seed rates: groundnuts and beans at 100kg/ha.
3. SSMS seed producer prices and ADMARC retail seed prices: taken from MOA price policy document (GOM, 1989).
4. Yields: groundnuts at 700kg/ha (average recorded in SSMS 1984/85 – 1986/87 according to Sibale and Mtambo (1989) – this is higher than in Malawi's official *Guide to Agriculture*); beans at 700kg/ha (average grain yield in *Guide*).
5. ADMARC storage and handling costs: 10% of cost of seed, as used in ADMARC's national seed storage and handling costings.
6. Labour: extra labour theoretically needed for planting and weeding but, as standard seed rates used, assumed needed only for weeding. Assumed weeding takes up approx. 33% of total time input normally and requirement is doubled under SSMS, so total labour input increased by 17%. Labour input figures per ha taken from AES (1987), as used in MOA price policy document, costed at minimum rural daily wage per hour, assuming 5 hour working day (as recommended in AES, 1987).
7. Transport: costed at MK0.03/kg for weight of inputs and produce, as used in MOA price policy document.
8. Field inspections: average price paid by NSCM to Seed Services for field visits to contract maize growers was MK14.60 per ha in 1989/90 (Seed Services records, NSCM records). This figure is used for SSMS as dealing with non-certified self-pollinated crops probably reduces costs but dealing with scattered plots increases them at the same time.
9. Gross margins: SACA credit package cost for commercial (not seed) packages taken; average small farmer yield (not higher seed yield); so transport costs reduced on both counts; commercial producer price.
10. Cost of seed in credit packages: the actual cost of this could not be calculated so the price charged to CDR farmers has been taken.

Index

access/availability, seed, 4, 19, 22, 35, 37, 38, 40, 42, 117, 119–20, 127, 130, 133, 145
   see also under individual countries
ACORD, 126
Actellic, 60
ACTIONAID, 67
adaptability, 27, 31, 35, 100, 112, 128
adjustment, structural, 1–3 *passim*, 16, 72, 92, 113
   see also reform, economic
advertising, 69, 87, 89, 115, 121, 123, 134
advice, 19, 38, 40, 42, 46, 60–1, 69, 81, 82, 84, 86, 89, 103, 115, 117, 118, 134
Africa Economic Digest, 45n9, 71n11, 119
agreements, 87
   Bipartite/Tripartite, 93, 103, 107, 108, 112, 114, 115, 133
agriculture, 1–3, 14–20, 29, 30, 39, 40, 43, 127–30, 132–3
   see also under individual countries
   commercialisation, 98, 101, 102, 104, 105, 111
   estate, 46, 54
   subsistence, 14, 15, 29, 47
Agriseeds, 112
AGRITEX, 101, 102
agro-ecology, 38, 40, 43, 45–6, 61–2, 67, 82, 87–8, 90, 92, 98, 104–5, 113, 125, 130–1
Ahmed, I., 15n5
aid, 9, 68, 73, 83, 85, 88, 102
   food, 17, 93
Ali, M., 15n4

Allan, A.Y., 128
Altieri, 23
Angola, 112
AOSCA, 149
Arndt, T., 15n5
Arnon, I., 15n5
ARPT, 17–20 *passim*, 22, 71
Ashworth, V.A., 153
Asia, 3, 6, 9–11 *passim*, 19, 144
associations, seed, 93, 94
   see also individual headings

Bangladesh, 11, 70
banks, 80
   seed, 23, 30, 32, 126
Barbier, E., 9
barley, 93, 144, 146
   Proctor, 146
barter, 21
Barton, L.V., 24
beans, 12, 16–18 *passim*, 24, 25, 27, 31, 126, 145, 149, 163
   see also under individual countries
   Nasaka, 55, 56
   Red Canadian Wonder, 54, 55
   Sapelekedwa, 55, 56
Bentley, F., 4
Berg, T., 24
biomass, 17
breeding, plant, 3, 5, 6, 8–11, 14, 17, 22, 27, 28, 31, 33, 120, 124, 129–35, 144–9 *passim*
   see also under individual countries
   Plant Breeding International, 66